Living Boldly & Dying Well

Dr. Deb Walters, B.S.W., M.Div., B.C.C., D.Min.
www.Drdebministries.com

Living Boldly & Dying Well
ISBN: Softcover 978-1-955581-11-0
Copyright © 2021 by Dr. Deb Walters

All rights reserved. No part of this book may be reproduced or transmitted in any form or by any means, electronic or mechanical, including photocopying, recording, or by any information storage and retrieval system, without permission in writing from the publisher.

Parson's Porch Books is an imprint of Parson's Porch & Company (PP&C) in Cleveland, Tennessee. PP&C is an innovative organization which raises money by publishing books of noted authors, representing all genres. Its face and voice is **David Russell Tullock** (dtullock@parsonsporch.com).

Parson's Porch & Company *turns books into bread & milk* by sharing its profits with the poor.

www.parsonsporch.com

Living Boldly & Dying Well

Contents

Dedication 7

Acknowledge 9

Dear Reader 11

Introduction 17
  First Things

Chapter One: 24
  Spiritual Attributes, Elements, and Disciplines

Chapter Two 62
  Physical

Chapter Three 73
  Emotional

Chapter Four 90
  Social

Chapter Five 96
  Cultural

Chapter Six 110
  Financial

Chapter Seven 118
  Vocational

Chapter Eight 129
  Last Things

Dedication

For my husband Don Walters: aka Papa Bear

For my friend Brenda Lewis

I can never thank either of you enough for encouragement, support, and sojourning with me in this clergy call of pastoral care for holism of wellness in mind-body-spirit.

I thank God for the laughter, loyalty, and unconditional love as we do life and ministry support and care together. We have lived as witnesses of one another that *Living Boldly and Dying Well* is about faith, hope, and love.

Don and Deb: Married 40 years

Debra and Brenda: Best of friends 32 years

Acknowledgement

The book cover is the work of art from Ellen McGaughey of Ellen's Art: https://www.ellens-art.com/

Ellen was a friend and neighbor when we lived in the Panhandle of Florida. We remained friends through Facebook. As I was praying about the cover of the book for *Living Boldly Dying Well*, I came upon a post Ellen showed of her painting something freeform after praying for the Holy Spirit to inspire her hands and give her art an expression from the soul. The moment I saw this work I felt moved by it. It reminded me of the internal work of the landscape of a soul. We had not seen each other face to face in over 20 years. We got to together while on a beach trip and discussed this amazing work. This art moved me by the colors, texture, and movement. Thank you, Ellen, for sharing your gift of painting and letting this work be the cover for my words shared for soul care from my soul.

This slide is from a PowerPoint on a seminar given on balancing the complexity of our holistic efforts to live a balanced life of faith with God-Self/Soul-Others. God's movement in the world is ever present if we would notice God, our own, others. The dance of daily rhythm or out of step is obvious to those with eyes to see and ears to hear.

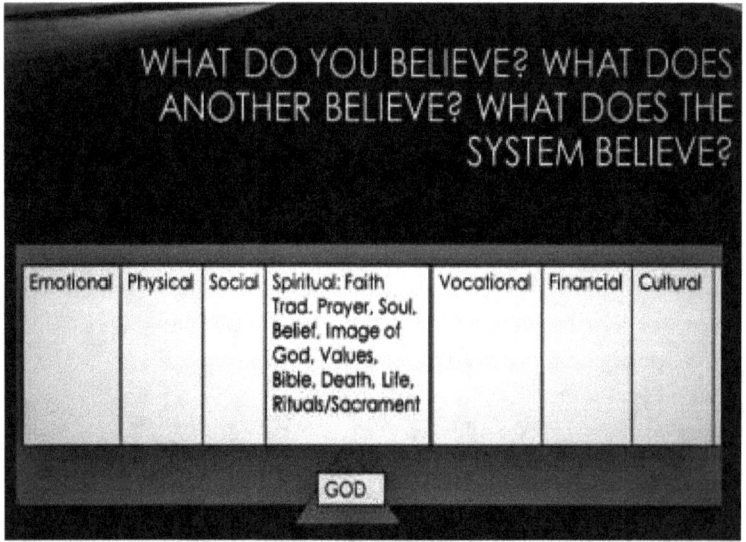

Dear Reader

This book of encouraging a life of awareness and interconnectedness to God, Self/Soul and Others began decades ago. There is a rhythm to life's seasons. There is an opening and closing to chapters of our life that has death like experiences, grief, gratitude, and literal goodbyes that end in a funeral. How do we join in this rhythm of living, grieving, counting our blessings, and dying contributions of experiences and interactions? Why do we believe what we believe? Are we able to believe what we believe without compromising our own or insulting another's? Is what we hold dear in our values and beliefs vetted with God's Word and Spiritual Wisdom? How can we know the joy and laughter of living and ignore the pain and loss in living too?

In what ways do we contribute to both sides of this wonder and wicked dispositions oozing into our spirit from external sources? Can we consider experiences from the wonder and wicked of life which inform our internal spirit of who we are from the inside out? Is there authenticity and congruency or are the masks of control, power, and faux love in shallow ways and means a survival mechanism of self-interests? Is the world a better place while we are here? Do we give more than we take? Do we love as God has loved us?

When I sit with a counselee, teach a class on wholeness and spiritual wellbeing, or biblical study, I encourage the ability to sit with a variety of questions. Questions hold the most important attribute within the very word question. The answers to any question rest in that word quest, which is the invitation to a journey. The quest for answers is in the very questions we are all prepared to ask. It takes courage to find the answers we are looking deep within ourselves where the answers live.

I confess I am a lifelong learner that has always investigated questions. Why do we do that? How true is that belief? If we live by our faith that sustains us; why do, we fear so much and grieve so poorly? If God is love; how are we defining love? Do I believe this or that because of my culture? What are my values and clarifications which influence those values from the effects of what is just or unjust? What is prayer and how important is it, really? Do we have freewill? If so, where in the story of us does it show up to reveal ourselves to ourselves? What does our spirituality have to do with our finances, physicality, vocation, social circles, emotions, and cultural nuances?

In this journey of words, stories, scriptures, and questions you will see me use human-divine because we are both. We forget that fact is laid out by God in the early chapters of Genesis and from the work of Jesus in his ministry teachings: but we are. In this read the term use of self/soul is also used throughout this mapping a spiritual life in Christian Spirituality. The purpose is to be clear that we do not have a soul tucked away and hidden in the gut of who we are until our last breath is released and the soul floats away out of the Nephesh of our being. That is but one characteristic of the soul's eternal movement from here to there of the leaving. Nephesh is the place deep within our belly that the Hebrew word offers the many meanings of the soul's character as person, body, beast, human, lust, mind, heart, creature, self, and ghost to name but a few words to describe a soul. The self is Eh-stem phonetically in Hebrew and speaks to the self or essence as bone. The self is a total package of flesh, bone, and essence/persona. The Greeks would treat our bodies, self, and bone as separated from the soul of a person. This compartmentalization has been a large part of why psychology, religions, and spirituality have struggled for centuries around moralism and humanism to name two isms that cost the soul of us by neglecting the soul's divinity attributes of 'let us make them in our image' (Gen. 1:26).

The Greek word for soul is psuche/psych and refers similarly to the Hebrew meaning of Nephesh as one's essence, bone, body, character, and being. When Jesus says, "My **soul** is overwhelmed with sorrow to the point of death. Stay here and keep watch with me." (Matthew 26:38) is an inclusiveness of his whole self and soul.

They are mingled and involved in the interconnectedness of his own mind-body-spirit. If our soul hurts, then our body hurts. If we treat our body with disregard and disrespect, then is it obvious we erase and disregard our soul too in the interconnected decisions of how we are willing to treat our own self/soul well or not well in the story of ourselves. If we treat our body-mind-spirit in harmonious balance and care of contentment no matter the circumstance then it gives credence to the term, 'it is well with my soul.'

When this read speaks of Christian Spirituality in terms of God-Self/Soul-Others; it is reflecting that the ways we define our understanding of God and living out of our own self/soul reflects how we will treat others and address others in our interconnected encounters. In the complexity of the human divine stories the details are neither black nor white in simplistic outcomes. The freewill we have to react and respond lives in the grayer areas of how we encounter and live with God, how we encounter and live with ourselves, and thus how we encounter and interact with others.

This book is an invitation to ask ourselves some questions. The quests within the questions can help you and I see what we believe about God, ourselves, and others. This read is a conversation that assumes the main reader is Christian. Christian Spirituality is at its simplistic defining a follower of Christ. And it, Christian Spirituality, builds a life on both the Jewish and Christian writing of scripture in Old/New Testament. Built on this foundation, Christian Spirituality seeks to live a 'whole and holy' life that has meaning, values, and beliefs that include informing and transforming us to grow and keep growing with our relationship with God. This includes a transcendence of knowing there is a Mystery to this God we will never put in a tidy box of owning this Creator as the created. We the created are always in awe and homage to the One who did the creating as our Creator. This Mysterious God is known by many names. Scripture speaks of God in the Judeo-Christian scriptures and it is Hagar, an Egyptian handmaid to Sarah/Abraham who names God first in scripture as a God who sees us. (El Roi)

Reader, I am going to refer to scripture, biblical stories, and spiritual layers taught by Christ and Disciples in the Old and New Testament that have formed, reformed, and transformed my own Christian Spirituality that is unashamedly foundational to this work and words offered to you as reader. I am not writing to convince you or myself on the image of God, who Jesus is in the 21st century mindset, or if there is a one size fits all group think for lockstep' sake in our Christian Spirituality. If that is what you are seeking in your quest in the questions; it will disappoint you.

However, if you are open to prayer, self/soul examination, and how to walk in this world with God, Self/Soul, and Others with a sense of spiritual contentment you may find the Kingdom of God within this journey leads to a deepening of what and how to be holy and whole in unholy moments that attempt to dismantle our wholeness. If so, you may find this the right book for the journey of a bold life with death or dying moments have regard and respect for both contributions.

Jesus spoke to this very spiritual concept in the kingdom of God among us, within us, and transforming us from the words of Jeremiah and Jesus himself. The journey from Old Testament to New for those who seek God in our daily lives is to seek the kingdom of God with us, for us, and within us. Throughout this read, you will notice a term of self/soul in the mix of explanations. My prayer and journey with the Holy One are to notice we poorly and erroneously compartmentalize and segregated our lives and thus divide our very sense of self from our soul and our soul from our self.

We are made in the image of God, thus there is a divinity of soulfulness and spirit within each of us as we maneuver in our human form. What impacts our humanity will affect our very soul and sense of self in persona at the same time. They are not separate entities. Our sense of self will impact our soul, and the maturing or arrested pretext of the soul will affect our very self. When we are hurt physically or emotionally, our very soul will hurt too. When our very soul is crushed and grieved, our body and personality of self will expose us to ourselves and others. They are interlinked and interlocked by our freewill choices of human-divine growth and Oneness with God, Self/Soul, and Others.

I hope you will notice the hospitality to come along on a journey to consider who is God? Not simply your understanding of God per your introduction to God. Who is God without our projections and assumptions from external experiences? What does the Holy Spirit disclose to you about God, Yourself/soul, and Others as you move in this one life?

Hopefully, the essence of hope, love, and faith from the Holy Spirit will be your tour guide through the questions. Maybe the outcome by the end of this read will feed your spirituality in Christianity to have room for grace, forgiveness, mercy, wisdom and gratitude which invites us to live bold lives with God, Self/Soul, Others. This way of being in the world allows us to die well when it is our turn to exit from this life to another with a legacy of faith worth living out and offering to the next generation.

Thank you, reader, for joining but one quest of spirituality in Christianity. I hope this journey through words, stories, and questions brings you joy, awareness, and spiritual tools for future journey's in living a life boldly and well in Christian Spirituality.

Peace and Grace Always, Dr. Deb

When we suffer, and we will, God suffers too.
When we dance, and we will, God dances too.
When we sing, and we will, God sings too.
When we laugh, and we will, God laughs too.
When we hurt, and we will, God hurts too.
Whatever we endure, or cause others to endure for encountering one another: God holds both and all.
And thus,
God still creates from the stories of us and our freewill.

Introduction

First Things

(Composite and photos by Dr. Deb)

"For as a person thinks within themselves, so they are" Proverbs 23:7.

"I am a big believer in that ritual can put us in touch with our spirituality" Sue Monk Kidd

Jesus replied: "'Love the Lord your God with all your heart and with all your soul and with all your mind." Matt: 22:37

Whatever faith tradition, family background, or cultural influence people are born into there is at some point an introduction to God. First impressions are important. We only get one shot at setting the tone for the job interview, the first date, or the encounter of a new beginning in a new school. We all remember those moments of first impressions. How often do we consider how God feels about his first introductions to us?

Was it a fiery God in an old wooden church back in a time of segregation? Did you meet God in the touch of goodnight prayers, stories read, and a tender kiss from a loving parent? Was God a mysterious entity in the smoke from canters, chants of Latin, and ornate rituals? Did God meet you in nature and overwhelm with creation's majesty? Was God there in the silence of an abyss that threatened to take over your life? Did God nourish you in a good meal with delightful laughter? Was God judgmental and harsh, with rules and laws clamoring for obedience by religious leaders? Were you ever introduced to God? Was God only a religious set of rules, cultural norm, or denominational doctrine? Does God seem cruel to you and indifferent to a hurting world? Does God show favoritism to some and left others in want?

How we meet someone affects our beliefs about them. We come to believe what they project, showed, stated, and offered to us. The encounter of others, our own experiences, and our own freewill around perceptions influences how we process our experiences and beliefs.

Over the years, I believe that the God of my childhood was a benevolent dictator. If I was good, then God is pleased with me. If something bad happened to me, then it was a punishment for something I must have done wrong. However, there was an experience in nature by age eight that became an anchor for me in the encountering of God as Creator that would awe me and give me roots with a God of Majesty and Mystery I could trust, and sense was around me and with me.

The God of my adolescence was a God I encountered in scripture through Jesus' words and ways from the book of Luke. Struggles through sexism, eating issues, and social injustice offered me a God that shows up in the pain, hurts, disappointments, and stoic determination to press onward.

The young adult God I came to know was one that offered spiritual investigation to hone beliefs by study. Study of human behavior, dance, photography, storytelling/biographies, scripture, literature, historical events, family dynamics, ethics, politics, personality traits, grief, death, and gratitude. This various and veracious study habits rested in the one spiritual discipline I valued the most and had built a relationship with God was through prayer.

This one value clarification was the glue for me through childhood to young adulthood. Prayer shaped my spiritual investigations to understand God more fully. Within my prayer life, I maneuvered through the ages and stages of my daily life. Today, I realize through study that I was naturally aware of God in the daily course of life, just as Ignatius had taught in the 1500s. He was one of thirteen children. He was wounded in battle. The recuperation experience introduced him to God amid suffering. He studied the life of Jesus and church saints of the time. This study leads to him establishing the Jesuits and spiritual direction care that would become known as contemplatives in action.

Now, I knew nothing about St. Ignatius in my early formative years, nor in my young adult years through thirty something. I was nearly forty years of age before my studies brought me to this connection that helped me to experience God as one who had known me better than I knew myself. This concept of contemplatives in action, more than resonates with me. There is a sense of knowing myself better with God and God with me in such a concept of being a contemplative individual who desires to do for others some soul caring.

These years of observing, studying, praying, and striving melted into a peace that passes all understanding. Over the years, my foundational belief in God rested in a prayer life grounded from study. The Ignatius' life was an inspirational find for me. Have you ever been in an organized faith, family, or culture that made you feel like a misfit more than belonging? The study of Ignatius puts a pin in the map of life that validated what was a natural personality affinity of being me. I resonated with Ignatius biography of meeting God in pain and suffering, the understanding of God through the study of Christ, and the offering of unceasing prayer feeds the spirituality of daily life with God.

It was an attitude and commitment to prayerfully noticing God moving in the day with me. What were my five senses and intuition of discernment with the Holy Spirit showing me in the movement of daily routines of school, chores, eating, jobs, events, and preparing the ordinary moments to have some extraordinary opportunities to notice God with me?

In my life there is a joy I get from movement of dance, photography, writing prayer poetry, and being in nature. I have memories of gratitude that my athletic days in dance and sports gave me joy and artistic glee in accomplishing a modern dance routine that told a story in movement or playing softball or golf and the thrill of a good shot that landed either of those types of balls where I had hoped it would go either from luck or good form. I would take either!

I would take a camera with me just about everywhere from age fourteen to present. I would seek the moment to capture a shot that would capture a memory, a story, or the beauty of nature. Ansel Adams was my favorite famous photographer growing up, and to this day I hold a love for well-done black and white photography. There is something about the contrasts of grays within the black and white that light does which speaks to me. Ever notice the beauty of God in nature? In black and white photography, I would naturally gravitate to the brightest of white and darkest of black in the shot and find the contrast speaks of giving clarity to the value that both shades of color compliment the other to shine. Without the dark the white is not as brilliant and without the brilliance of the white the dark could become foreboding and dismissed as nothing. There is much that Carl Jung would say about the light and dark within us as human beings. The balance of each side of us is the human divine struggle.

However, in photography it is the depth that comes in the shadings of subtle grays that transition the white and black landscape that awakens something spiritual within me. In the gray there is something mysterious and forming that transforms us if we look closer at the Master Designers work. The color gray spiritually is about seeking balance. Biblically, gray is the color of ashes, and represents Lent, fasting and prayer. There is something in the gray that speaks of God to me who is wooing us to notice that the shading of life in gray is neutral because it is a place of pondering and possibilities of what we can know, do, and be with God in the light and dark moments of our life. But it is in the gray where we must decide how we will live in the tensions of life's offering us events of brilliance and awe verses the events of disappointments, despairs, and devastations. In the gaps where gray lives are the space of calm, discernment, and decisions that will tie meaning making and freewill choosing's to what one will do with the black and white moments that life offers us all in the human-divine race.

Ansel Adams: Mt. McKinley

I like ordinary moments of a routine day that goes well; I checked the duties on the list off, and the outcome of the day is never a rut for me. Dishes have to be done, so I enjoy feeling the warm to hot water running over my fingers and giving my joints a warm soothing sensation while a chore is being completed. When I cannot open a jar or bottle cap because of my hands, there is a willing husband or kitchen tool available to assist. In the years of practicing an attitude of gratitude all roads rest at the crossroads of attitude, character, freewill, and owning one's own story from the choices made from these three contributions of attitude, character, and freewill. What has been yours? What have been the attitude, character, and freewill encounters with others? Where are you in those gray shades and tones of pondering the possibility of how you hold light and dark in equal regard? How can prayer, discernment, owning one's choices benefit you in living a spiritual journey in a human existence? Who is God to you? When do you seek God's presence in the ordinary routine days?

In this journey of words, stories, scriptures, and questions you will see me use human-divine because we are both. We forget that fact is laid out by God in the early chapters of Genesis and from the work of Jesus in his ministry teachings: but we are. In this read the term use of self/soul is also used throughout this mapping a spiritual life in Christian Spirituality. The purpose is to be clear that we do not have a soul tucked away and hidden in the gut of who we are until our last breath is released and the soul floats away out of the Nephesh of our being. That is but one characteristic of the soul's eternal movement from here to there of the leaving event at death.

Nephesh is the place deep within our belly that the Hebrew word offers the many meanings of the soul's character as person, body, beast, human, lust, mind, heart, creature, self, and ghost to name but a few words to describe a soul. The self is Eh-stem phonetically in Hebrew and speaks to the self or essence as bone. The self is a total package of flesh, bone, and essence/persona. The Greeks would treat our bodies, self, and bone as separated from the soul of a person. This compartmentalization has been a large part of why psychology, religions, and spirituality have struggled for centuries around moralism and humanism to name two isms that cost the soul of us by neglecting the soul's divinity attributes of 'let us make them in our image' (Gen. 1:26).

The Greek word for soul is psuche/psych and refers similarly to the Hebrew meaning of Nephesh as one's essence, bone, body, character, and being. When Jesus says, "My **soul** is overwhelmed with sorrow to the point of death. Stay here and keep watch with me." (Matthew 26:38) is an inclusiveness of his whole self and soul. They are mingled and involved in the interconnectedness of his own mind-body-spirit. If our soul hurts, then our body hurts. If we treat our body with disregard and disrespect, then is it obvious we erase and disregard our soul too in the interconnected decisions of how we are willing to treat our own self/soul well or not well in the story of ourselves. If we treat our body-mind-spirit in harmonious balance and care of contentment no matter the circumstance then it gives credence to the term, 'it is well with my soul.'

When this read speaks of Christian Spirituality in terms of God-Self/Soul-Others; it is reflecting that the ways we define our understanding of God, experience ourselves reflects how we will treat others and address others in our interconnected encounters. In the complexity of the human divine stories the details are neither black nor white in simplistic outcomes. The freewill we have to react and respond lives in the grayer areas of how we encounter and live with God, how we encounter and live with ourselves, and thus how we encounter and interact with others.

Chapter One:

Spiritual Attributes, Elements, and Disciplines

God is Love: 1 John 4: 7-21

Many speak of God as a God of love. This description needs a defining about the word love. Definitions and projections around wordings take on meaning that may or may not be accurate.

Our definition of love rests in emotional connections of a feeling. The feelings of intensity for those we are in a relationship based on the label we have with them will influence the various degrees of where this love goes when it establishes around a feeling.

The connections of parent to child, child to parent, lovers, friends, relatives, and strangers will vary on the encounters, feelings, and expectations that inform the love one holds between them. This is often conditional loving of quid pro quo and what has transpired or not transpired between the human relating.

In our Western culture this use of the word love has a worn-out usury, and it has lost its virility. I love that outfit, ice cream, show, and so on goes the list of things or events that reduce the love of another human being to that of a thing or event which reduces the intimacy of what love means to distinguish or elevate.

This word is also a weapon of withholding and controlling another person, which ironically exhibits and exposes how unloving another is when love is not worth the speaking or the showing. I noticed years ago several of my peers were having issues with their children, not saying the words of love to them as a parent. It stung their heart to have their child refuse to say, "I love you." It had happened to me too, with one of my own. And this befuddled me and even angry at the immaturity of such behavior but chalked it up to immaturity that would pass as the adolescent stage is not forever: God forbid!

One day a coworker at work was on the phone with her teenage daughter and I heard her demand the words of love from her daughter. She had said the words of love to her young daughter and expected a respectful courtesy of reciprocity in closing the phone conversation. The daughter withheld the words, and the mother explained that if she wanted her to keep doing all that she does for her as mom and she cannot give a simple kind retort of love then the helping and providing to go above and beyond for her would end! The girl relented, and the conversation ended with anger and frustration more than the words spoken would reflect. There were ground rules and respectful declarations of a gauntlet to explain to an arrogant teenager who was withholding a sentiment important in a parent child/child parent relationship. This mom was also taking this moment to stand up for herself as a human-divine being. How dare this child welcome the trips, clothes, support activities, and doing life well by this child in time, money, and energy for her greater good and she cannot show or say the words of love? Both were reacting, and it is easy to opine an opinion on another in their demands for words or the withholding of words to control one another.

Whatever we think about this scenario, we too have expectations of words, deeds, and utilizations of how love manifests itself in our relating. Most talk about love in terms of conditional and unconditional love. And these are two states of being that are contributions to love.

They often characterize God as the only one who loves us all unconditionally. Nothing changes the fact that God loves us all, flaws and all. There is nothing we can do to make God not love us no matter the behaviors, or mistakes made. True. And no human being can ever understand this level of love, for we have all put conditions on whether we love or do not love another. Not true.

Love is an action of being, not an emotion or fleeting feeling. I knew when this mother was holding her daughter accountable for her immaturity in withholding the words, there was a deeper matter at play. If she let her behave and keep on behaving with such mean girl antics to use emotional blackmail on her, then where does such antics stop. Will she use such manners of withholding to control her husband one day? Will she play games with words and ways on her own children one day? Will she misuse her friends and siblings with conditional attitudes to control them? Will she sabotage her own self-respect by being disrespectful to others in playing emotional and mental games with words of love withheld and actions that will follow her as shallow, superficial, and grow into a silly child inside a full-grown woman's body one day?

This mother knew her daughter loved her. She did not need hearing the words literally said to sooth her own emotional needs or ego. She went into the actions of love and loving her daughter enough to call her out on her immaturity that this cannot be the way she uses a relationship to get what she wants and then mistreats the person with disdain by withholding the action of love expressed with a lack of gratitude, respectfulness, appreciation, and regard.

God never stops loving any of us. And any decent parent will always love their own unconditionally, too. All friendships, marriages, and working relationships have a love element of unconditional attributes, but the relationship has some conditions. Even God requires conditions for the relationship to be strong and vital. God can love us, even if we do not love God. God will always love, even if the relationship is not functioning and involved. Ask any parent of an estranged child and they will usually speak of unconditional love, but the relating and connecting with one another has some agreed upon conditions if it is to be a healthy and vital relationship for both parties. And when the action of love is a one-way street, then the relationship is out of balanced and not authentically a healthy one, full of God's idea of 'love one another.'

The verse in 1 John 4: 20 says, "If anyone says, "I love God," and hates his brother, he is a liar; for he who does not love his brother whom he has seen cannot love God whom he has not seen. 21 And this commandment we have from him: whoever loves God must also love his brother."

This verse reminds us that the authenticity to the action of love is about the ability to love another through trust. Now, let me be honest here. None of us will literally trust everyone we encounter in our families, faith community, work settings, and so on. The trust is about trusting ourselves and trusting God to give us the insight of healthy boundaries, limitations, conditions, and dust off our feet moments with those we know we can still love with or without being in literal relationships with some people. There are those we encounter who are not trustworthy with our name, personhood, nor can we do life with them because of the toxicity or conditions of critique they emit into the encounter with them. However, in God's way of loving, we can love them from afar and/or with limitations.

The prodigal story is one of my favorites in the book of Luke. I would invite anyone to take time to read the many messages and words that this narrative offers in Chapter 15 of the book of Luke. There are many nuggets of wisdom to discern and discuss. For our purpose, I would like to go to the point regarding the eldest son, who was good and faithful to his father and highly judgmental of his wayward younger brother. Jesus is speaking in a parable that offers religious leaders and those who say they love God to stop and reflect on how skewed their version of love had made them bitter and rigid with others. The elder brother is the symbol of danger in all of us who live for a faith by law and keeping rituals as a way of doing love for God, but not actually being God's version of love or love in action within ourselves. When we cannot and will not say the words of love or show love to another, then we do not love God either. How could we love God when we do not love ourselves enough to be open to receiving love from God?

The elder son in this story is the dutiful son, the one who follows the religious laws, and has a heart of stone toward his brother. Jesus is pointing to the hypocrisy that is closing their soul to become small and erased by the lack of love held for God and thus others. For one does not fake genuine love for any length of time.

In this story, the father saw the prodigal from far off and ran to him. Now in the story, the father agreed to let the boy do what he knew would most likely be the outcome. When the prodigal left home in this story, the father did not chase after him or try to change his mind. He loved him but loved him enough to let him figure out some things for himself. The young man would squander his resources from his life choices. He would find himself regretful in his attitude towards home and his father. He would decide to go back and ask to be received back into the family fold as a servant in his father's house. But while on his way to return; the father went out to greet and welcome the boy back. The elder brother did not rush in to greet his brother upon hearing of the return. That speaks volumes of the rigid rules and judgementalism of a hardened heart that has no room for love when pride is in the faithful one who follows the rules, didn't create havoc for his father, and pulled his own weight in the family business. He did not however have an attitude of gratitude, unconditional love, or show a desire to enjoy life with his father or his sibling. He simply made no waves and followed the rules while harboring hard feelings toward his brother and the father. Scripture reveals the eldest brother's internal disposition.

But God sees the internal secret places in the heart and soul of all humankind and is not fooled by the austere surface of what appears good and seems in line with one that would love God, thus his own father, and his brother as he does life with them. God is fully aware of who loves him and out of that love for the Holy One, a person can honestly love all others with or without a relationship. However, if a loving relationship is to be rich and real in its love, there are attributes that will soften and condition the relating with the fruit of God's Holy Spirit. Jesus said, "you shall know them by their fruits…" (Matt. 7:16).

So, if love, in this context, is about the tap root of depth that feeds every aspects of our self /soul then we must take to heart what Jesus said about fruit as a metaphor for noticing who actually loves, who loves poorly and conditionally, and who loves like a wolf in sheep's clothing hoodwinking others who fall for charm and lies. We will know them by their fruit is key to self/soul awareness about who honestly loves and loves well as Jesus modeled from His Father God.

Love in this vein is about a relationship built on the fruit attributes listed in Galatians 5 and contributions of loyalty, character, trust, freedom, autonomy, revealing ethics, ownership of one's own choices, maturity, courage, altruism, and reciprocal 'love'.

God as love is an all-in love for you and me. When we love like this, then the love as an action verb which moves in these attributes and being 'known' by such fruitful outcomes. Jesus models this love. Chapter seventeen of John is the last prayer of Christ and describes the Oneness that his love has for God and God for Him and for the disciples. Then he prays for the future believers who will follow him and love God as their Holy One and welcomed into this spiritual dance of inclusion.

John 17: 20-26 "My prayer is not for them alone. I pray also for those who will believe in me through their message, 21 that all of them may be one, Father, just as you are in me and I am in you. May they also be in us so that the world may believe that you have sent me. 22 I have given them the glory that you gave me, that they may be one as we are one — 23 I in them and you in me—so that they may be brought to complete unity. Then the world will know that you sent me and have loved them even as you have loved me.

24 "Father, I want those you have given me to be with me where I am, and to see my glory, the glory you have given me because you loved me before the creation of the world.

25 "Righteous Father, though the world does not know you, I know you, and they know that you have sent me. 26 I have made you known to them and will continue to make you known in order that the love you have for me may be in them and that I may be in them."

Now this level of love was described in the Old Testament too, in the metaphor of a plumb line. A plumb line is a tool that reveals in building terms what is crooked and what is made straight. Scripture speaks to God's desire in His love for us, for Israel, in following Christ that we are to be His Children of light and love that strives for what is good, trustworthy, and true over evil and crooked selfish ways.

Study Isaiah 28:16-17, Amos 7:8, and II Timothy 3:16-17. These are but a few references to God's expectations for holy lives that love God, love of one's own self/soul, and love for another.

In John 15: 9-17 we have "As the Father has loved me, so have I loved you. Now remain in my love. 10 If you keep my commands, you will remain in my love, just as I have kept my Father's commands and remain in his love. 11 I have told you this so that my joy may be in you and that your joy may be complete. 12 My command is this: Love each other as I have loved you. 13 Greater love has no one than this: to lie down one's life for one's friends. 14 You are my friends if you do what I command. 15 I no longer call you servants, because a servant does not know his master's business. Instead, I have called you friend, for everything that I learned from my Father I have made known to you. 16 You did not choose me, but I chose you and appointed you so that you might go and bear fruit—fruit that will last—and so that whatever you ask in my name, the Father will give you. 17 This is my command: Love each other."

Real love takes on the action-packed ways of seeking the Oneness with this God of love that Jesus taught about on the Sermon on the Mount, in the Lord's Prayer, and multiple messages and parables for those who had ears to hear and eyes to see how a daily life with God calls out human-divine ways to live. The ordinariness of daily life with attention to walking and talking with the Holy One we call God is to live extraordinarily awakened and alive each day.

If we would simply notice God in the mix of doing daily life, we can witness the movement of God's love in the world within ourselves, from others, and see love in action in everyday circumstances. If we pay attention, we can be witnesses and participants in God's love in action in extraordinary moments that live on to become inspirational history. If we would slow down enough to pay attention in the hamster wheel of life there is a vast amount of love in the world being shown and offered in compassion, contributions, acts of valor, routine steadiness, and dependability.

"If I speak in the tongues of men or of angels, but do not have love, I am only a resounding gong or a clanging cymbal. 2 If I have the gift of prophecy and can fathom all mysteries and all knowledge, and if I have a faith that can move mountains, but do not have love, I am nothing. 3 If I give all I possess to the poor and give over my body to hardship that I may boast, but do not have love, I gain nothing.

4 Love is patient, love is kind. It does not envy; it does not boast; it is not proud. 5 It does not dishonor others; it is not self-seeking; it is not easily angered; it keeps no record of wrongs. 6 Love does not delight in evil but rejoices with the truth. 7 It always protects, always trusts, always hopes, always perseveres.

8 Love never fails. But where there are prophecies, they will cease; where there are tongues, they will be stilled; where there is knowledge, it will pass away. 9 For we know in part and we prophesy in part, 10 but when completeness comes, what is in part disappears. 11 When I was a child, I talked like a child; I thought like a child; I reasoned like a child. When I became a man, I put the ways of childhood behind me. 12 For now we see only a reflection as in a mirror; then we shall see face to face. Now I know in part; then I shall know fully, even as I am fully known.

13 And now these three remain: faith, hope and love. But the greatest of these is love." I Cor. 13. We know this as the love chapter in the New Testament.

Many of these verses and chapters of scripture are not merely proof of God's love. They display a defining of love as an action out of deep abiding commitment and character traits of a God none of us will be able to fully comprehend nor put in a box of faith traditions and own a Holy God. We can meet God in places of denominational and religious heritages, but none can say they own something as Holy as God. Each strives to give sacred space and sacramental moments of worshiping and giving homage to the Holy One who is Creator. But we must never forget, we are the created ones to this Creator we named God since the days of Genesis. God's love put in motion the willingness to create and give us life and then asked humanity to join in co-creating with God.

What if we stopped and examined ourselves around the ability to love in action? How do we encounter God in the Old and New Testament? Do we encounter God's own love actions in scriptures and find a God of love is not simplistic, shallow, or emotionally laden with sappy sentiments? Are we willing to co-create with God in the living out of our lives? God as love is complex, deeply grounded in endlessness, and never based and fed by fleeting emotions. God as love is an action, character traits of spiritual fruit, and never ends.

What would our own Oneness in the spiritual cosmic dance of love in action look like if we honestly valued the love God has for us as individual self/souls?

What if we loved ourselves in authenticity and genuine respect for being one of God's children of light? Would we then find it as natural as breathing in and out to love one another?

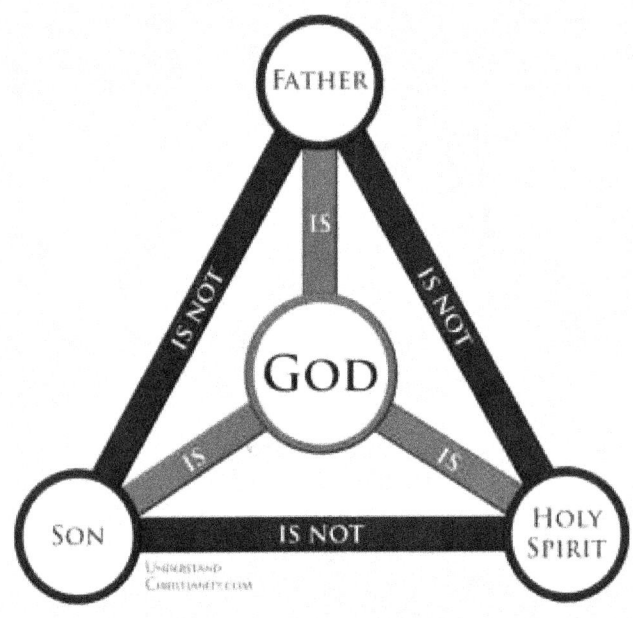

(Cite and Credit to: Understanding Christainity.com)

This is the best symbolism of explanation of the Oneness with God's Trinitarian attributes I have found. Thus, I am spiritually wooed to consider this Christian Spirituality as a way of being, living out our lives boldly, and walking with this Holy One in the daily; this God of love invites us to activate authentic love. We will know how authentic our love language with God holds by the way we will treat others and allow ourselves to be handled by others. The relationship which uses regard and respect within our God walk is revealed and reflected in how we hold ourselves in authenticity of healthy love of self/soul and how we treat others in similar respectful regards too.

(Concept of interconnected interactions by Dr. Deb)

To love God, Self/Soul, and Others well in life is to acknowledge how interconnected this love language binds us, affects us, fractures us, or breaks us apart by the choices of freewill we used to move in this world.

When I was growing up the church taught that to have real spiritual joy in our lives, we were to put Jesus first, others second, and ourselves last. This sounds noble on the surface but the motive to address selfishness in this theory of spiritual wellness is to offer unwellness to a spirituality of becoming a rug others walked on, use, and victimize a self/soul into being an enabler, codependent, and disrespected by others. Jesus never modeled that loving others meant your own self/soul was to put up with relationships that expected to 'be first' before your own sanity and soul care.

Jesus also said do not cast pearls (Matt. 7:6) and dust off your feet (Matt. 10:14). Jesus loved everyone as God did and does. Jesus did not stay in unhealthy relating situations and beg people to be loving or fair. As patient as God is with loving all humanity, God does not beg us to love and respectfully be in relationship with God. We choose.

Thus, I have found in my journey of spiritual health in an unholy moment in this world is to heed from God's love to seek the uniquely and wonderfully made me that God loves (Psalms 139). Who am I at my better and best self/soul that is congruent and authentic with God and myself? Who are you at your better and best self/soul that is congruent and authentic with God and yourself?

Once a standard of love between God and self/soul is forged, then there is a well of love from which to encounter others. Sometimes the best way to love God, self/soul, and others is to have some healthy doses of wisdom, boundaries, limitations, or no encounter at all for the sake of spiritual wellness to be maintained. Genuine love for God, self/soul, and others is not about everything is acceptable and good if we just love more from some emotionalism disposition. That would be naivete.

We live in a fallen and flawed world that has its fair share of evil and suffering in the world. Let us not fool ourselves either. Humankind down through the ages has done some remarkable and inspirational contributions to making the world a better place. However, humankind has also taken part in bringing hurt and harm to one another in deep wrenching ways too. And no one gets a pass. We all come into this world with the great capacity to do great love in this world, and we all have the great capacity to do harm and are complicit in evil and suffering whether or not we acknowledge such participation.

And while we can talk of God's love and God is love and define and redefine the concepts of this love as an action in the world that addresses evil and suffering stories; this love is also a reflective mirror that reveals that love is no small action when it requires us to die for others, forgive another, sacrifice for others, fight for others, hold another accountable, give to another, show up for others, challenge another, and receive the reciprocity of loves tough and tender sides which flows into the Oneness described in Jesus' prayer in John 17.

To love others the way God loves is to be in sync with God and our own self/soul awareness in order to love well unconditionally but the relating may come with conditions to remain authentically healthy for all concerned in the relating. God never models that he chases people down to love Him or force doing life with a Holy One. All are invited in hospitality to the relationship with unconditional love. However, there are also times that Jesus told his followers then and us now in scripture that we are not required to cast pearls (Matt. 7:6) and dust of feet when not welcomed Matt. 10:14) is to shake off where one is not wanted. Love at this level is about forgiving and letting go without hatred or apathy but remaining in love.

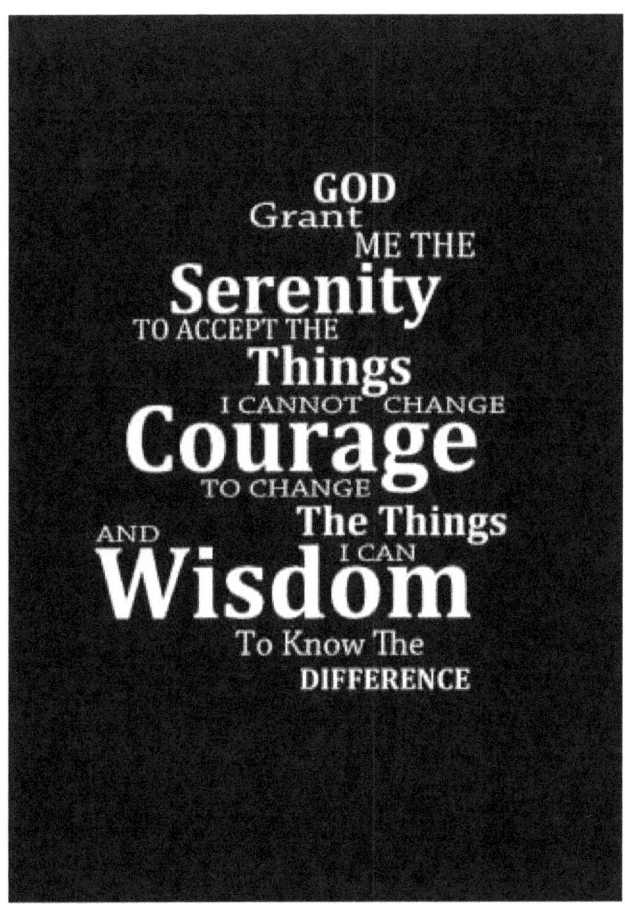

Aspects of Prayer

Conversation, which is what prayer is, allows for God's layers of love to be activated into action and deepened in the relationship. How can anyone love another they never talk with or rarely talk or listen to? Notice the use of the word 'with' rather than to talk to or talk at. Do you like one-way conversations with someone that just talks at you or talks to you but doesn't wait to hear your point of view or concern in a situation? How close would that friendship or relationship become? How stable will such a marriage remain? How trustworthy would you feel toward a child that demands a parent be there to serve them on their terms? How helpful is it to talk at a child and never explain the why in a request? But don't we do that to one another? How well do those dialogues and conversations go given the one-way laundry list of 'to do's' or the wish list of giving one's case for getting their way or throw away someone for not getting their way?

The way we converse with one another is often the very ways in which we dialogue with God. And we have the audacity to be affronted when we feel unheard or angry that God is not our personal servant or Santa Claus giving us our wish list. No relationship is worth much when the dialogue is a one-way street of give me, do this, do that, you're never there for me, if you love me, and on and on goes the tirade of blame, anger, frustration, and withholding of thanks and 'love you' words and ways for all the good that is in your life.

Many speak to God's ability to take our anger and immaturity in shallow prayers, and that is true. However, God did not allow Job or Job's friends to get away with an ongoing diatribe of arrogant opining about Job, God, or the grief in the situation in Job's life. Eventually, there was a line in the sand moment of enough is enough and stop it!

Read the book of Job and find how God responded. Since God is Holy and is glad to enjoy our company in the Oneness dance of doing life together; then God is hoping we will choose the deeper ways of love and feed our soul to grow into a holiness and holy way of living out our humanity with more essence of our spirituality maturing along the lifespan.

Scripture reveals that prayer is the constant openness and awareness that God is with us, for us, and available to us to speak with unceasing and unending sense of presence.

In Genesis Abraham interacts, negotiates, complains, and trusts God. Throughout the Old Testament we see this prayerful conversing with God and God's people over covenants (Gen. 12:1-

3; Gen 16:10), warring with other nations (Genesis 14:17-20; I Samuel 17:1-58; Judges 4: 1-24), being barren (Genesis 11:30; 25:21; 29:31; 1 Samuel 1: 11), dealing with family cultural dynamics (Genesis 19; 22; 25: 19-34; 29-31; 34; 38; and 49), sibling rivalry (Genesis 4; 37), grief (Book of Job), being in exile (Book of Esther; Isaiah; Jeremiah; Daniel), and in death (Job 1: 20-22; 2 Samuel 12: 18-20; Genesis 23:1-2; 25:9; 35:27-29; 49:30 and 50: 13)

These are but a few narrative stories that lay the groundwork of how God and human beings related in doing life with God, within themselves, and with others.

In the New Testament, the human interaction of conversing with God, self/soul, and others in narratives of life continues. We find a mutual agreement to have a covenant with God in (Luke 1:34; Matt. 1: 18-25; Luke 1:5-2:20; Luke 1: 5-17) warring with other nations (Mark 13: 7-8; Matt. 8: 5-10; Luke 3:14; Acts 10:1-6; Matt. 5: 38-45) Being Barren (Luke 1:6) Dealing with family dynamics (Mark 3: 31-35; Mark 6:4; Luke 9: 46-49) Sibling Rivalry (1 John 3:15-17; 1 Cor. 13: 4-6; Luke 15: 11-32; Gal. 5: 20-27) Grief (Matt. 5:4; Matt. 11:28; John 14: 27; Romans 8: 38-39; 2 Cor.1: 3-4; Rev. 14:13) Being in exile (Luke 10: 25-37; John 4: 1-42; Luke 17: 11-19; Mark 7: 24-29) and in death (John 11; Matt. 9: 18-26; Luke 23: 26-43)

The relationship we hold with God depends on our own participation within our own freewill. The relationship we hold within ourselves depends on our own participation in knowing ourselves. The relationship we hold with others depends on our willingness to take part in understanding another. Each of these relationships is weak or strong based on our freewill choice to choose to relate through the action of love, not an emotive disposition of fleeting feelings.

What we believe about God shapes our prayers. The scriptures previously offered and a myriad of others through the Old and New Testament solicits the powerful influence and function of utilizing prayer. The telling of the story reveals the needed prayer. The way one prays can reveal the deeper story of the one praying. When I read the Genesis stories, there is an amazing scope of seeking, asking, and knocking to know God and be known by God through the story.

When I read the book of Job, there is a deep anguish need to work out, pray out, and grieve out the pain of lament and loss with God, self/soul, and others.

When I read the book of Psalms, there is a treasure of stories within David's prayer poetry to see the wonder and wicked done in daily living taken to a Holy God. The Psalms capture the never-ending human condition of a God that goes with us in our daily existence if we would but notice. Psalms captures not only the story of an individual, but the community and a nation too.

The New Testament stories are full of the same understanding of humans seeking, knocking, and asking of God to be with them in their story. In the crevasses of many prayers offered and the sacred stories shared from scripture, there is a parallel process where the story crosses paths with our own. We can relate to the story and the prayer needed.

If I am to believe in a God who goes with us in daily lives; then we can sense God in not only the stories of ancestors' words in scripture but in our own. God is in the details of our theological autobiographies according to author Tim Eberhardt in *Story Telling and Pastoral Care*. When we pray and find that connection to the Divine, there is an opportunity to listen to your life. It is within the sense of our very being we tap into words with the Holy One in Three and notice our spiritual mirror reflecting to us our emotions, personality, habits, cultural influences, family history, and values clarified.

Often, we live in a prayer disposition of why something happened, and when will God answer our petition. The deeper word to explore in prayer with God is the question of How.

How do you see this matter, God? How do I carry this hard story? How are we to address this situation? How long do we wait for closure on a matter?

Holy One, how do I help in this story or be still so as not to hinder this matter further? The question of how in our prayers is healthier and far more helpful to our spiritual-human makeup than the crazy making quest on why.

The biblical narratives and our own stories are full of the juxtaposition of what healthy love versus unhealthy love looks like and how the outcomes are experienced and lived out. We can love out of an empathic, harmonious, nurturing, and healing kind of love for one another. When we see these outcomes, there is a joy in the interconnect delight of a win-win-win attribute and contribution to a beautiful ending of a beautiful storyline in the lives of each player involved, with God, Self/Soul, and Another/Others. However, we are often shown and experience the messiness of lives and a love (unhealthy) that breeds unkind control, manipulation, codependency, and a lack of respect as one uses another in the name of love.

The dictionary defines freewill to be about the independent choosing between options and the actions we will freely choose in addressing a situation or relationship by our own choosing. This concept of freewill is dependent and/or influenced by the attributes of responsibility, guilt, praise, sin, positive or negative experiences, and vulnerability to name a few influencers. The complexity of freewill is as intricate and challenging as trying to put God in a box with a denominational stamp and claim this one-dimensional label is God. Likewise, freewill is a complex gift from God. Often it feels like God gave human-divine beings the keys to a fast car and we crash it with our choices, or we enjoy it with great freedom and delight. Likewise, freewill as gift is like God giving us the keys to a fine home and our freewill destroys it and trashes the good with our human-divine choices or we are grateful and wise to the value of keys to a kingdom home and cherish it enough to protect it with a deep abiding love that flourishes on trust, respect, enjoyment, laughter, and making amazing memories with all who come through the front door and stay awhile.

To understand our relationship with God, self/soul, and others, we need to consider these definitions that color our understanding of God, our knowing ourselves/soul, and aware of another and others. Freewill is one foundational attribute and ingredient to having a loving relationship with God, self/soul, and others or not. Freewill is often not challenged enough to mature and grow into the treasure God gave to not only the first human-divine beings in the Creation story; but to every self/soul that has been given breath since.

How do we master an awareness to commune with God in prayer as a search for authenticity of ourselves? One of my favorite verses for such a reflective mirror is in the scripture from II Timothy 1:7, "for God did not give us a spirit of fear/timidity, but a spirit of power, love, and self-discipline/control." This verse is impactful when we consider the contrasting of dark and light fruit from Galatians 5:20-23.

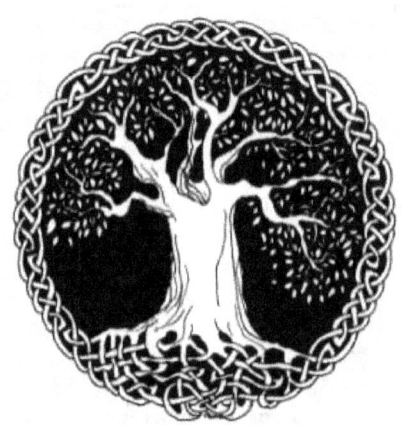

"God did not give us a spirit of fear but a spirit of love, power, self-control/discipline." 2 Tim. 1:7.

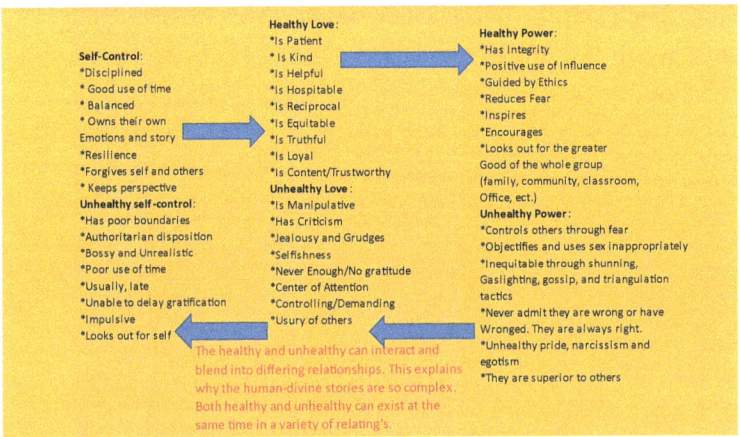

Imagine putting God's Spirit in the mix of us with God- our own self/soul- encountering others. We get to use our own freewill to carve out the life we have in the story of us as we each contribute and use how we choose to love, exercise our own power, and use self-control in our own story.

We see this played out from the beginning of the human-divine encounter since the Garden of Eden story in Genesis. This choosing of the fruit of the spirit and encountering God, self/soul, and others remains true today. It is not only the human condition but the human-divine connection too.

Some of my favorite scriptures that support this, 'in the beginning', story lives in Galatians 5: 20-27 and in II Tim. 1:7. These Galatian verses compare the attributes of the dark and light fruit that affect our relating with God, self, and others. The dark fruit needs little defining. We have within our human condition been overwhelmingly affect and/or have taken part in the easy opportunities. It is easy to be selfish and self-serving in the agenda that avarice, slander, malice, envy, quarrelsome, jealousy, and sexual misuse of another can offer.

These darker fruit attributes in relating to God, self/soul, and others rest in the hurt and harm that fear offers. If the spirit of 'light' fruit reflects our self/soul condition of spiritual strength and wellness; then sadly, the 'dark' fruit listed in Galatians 5 reflects the weaknesses and unwellness of a self/soul moving in the world too. Remember, the analogy and symbolism of gray in the photography work of black and white contrasts? It is here in this moment that we can see that it is fear and false pride that led a self/soul into those dark fruit places. But, somewhere in the story of them are opportunities to pray and seek in the gray matter of the moment to move. The Holy Spirit of God will assist us to move from dark to light by removing the fear and lies that false pride tricks and hoodwinks us. Prayer is our conduit to getting unstuck from the quagmire of regret, blame, and excuses that fear and false pride took us into the woods with dark fruit.

My paternal grandmother taught me how to can and preserve fruits and vegetables from her garden. When I became a mother of three children, I wanted to continue to help her in her canning season and offer the children an opportunity to see how preserving one's own food on the farm used to be a way of life. Every July we carved out time to have this adventure back to the country life in that old farmhouse. Peach picking time is about scorching sun, stoves, and spices leaving us sweaty and sticky at the end of a full day of canning. Picking, sorting, and preparing bushels of peaches into the usage they will become is one step of the process. The best peaches became spiced peaches while the better peaches became pie filling and the good enough for jelly come from the leftover peelings. I would put these peelings through a press that squeezed out every drop of juice and pulp of fruit for the jelly journey they would become on the hot stove. It would fill the kitchen air with spices, sugar, and peaches.

Isn't that how the fruit of God's Spirit works? The opportunity to take all the layers of our best, better, good, and flawed sides of our self and pressed out and made into something delicious and wonderfully made. (Ps. 139)

The fruit of the spirit from God in the verses from Galatians comes after a long list of darker fruits. The fruit of Holy Spirit is love, joy, peace, perseverance/forbearance, kindness, goodness, faithfulness, gentleness, and self-control. If we do not know the actual meaning of these words in original context, we will project our 20th and 21st century terminology onto them and be misguided on our human-divine journey.

Galatians 5 fruit of Spirit meaning:

A **love** that is God infused is to show and offer concern for others and their wellbeing. This adds to the spirit of **joy** that recognizes the favor of grace. This offers a **peace** that has a sense of God's wholeness that binds us as an individual with a peace of mind and wholeness we would want for others. These first three fruits of the spirit offer in **long suffering and perseverance** a way of being divinely patient with others while we remain steadfast and unwavering in our divine devotion to God.

Our **kindness** in the spirit's fruit is no weakness or weak attribute. This kindness offers real usefulness and helpfulness to others without being cruel to another or being treated cruelly by others. There is no English wording which honestly expresses this divine kindness accurately. The closest concept is that of 'do no harm to others or self.' Our English understanding is that of mutual regard and mutual respect in equality. Thus, to do no harm to another is equally valid to do no harm to yourself. This is a kindness attribute that shines on the need to remove selfish motives, mistreatment to self and others, and to rid ourselves and practices of civility with others of the dark fruit that rests in many injustices of disregard and disrespect of self and others. This spiritual standard of kindness is closely akin to the spiritual standard of goodness.

We only find this fruit of **goodness** in those that are true believers in God's desire for us to be of moral and virtue dispositions that are not of self-righteousness but humbleness to being true to God and self/soul. This goodness rests in humility, which is not about being a doormat of niceness but about genuine authenticity of congruency. The internal self/soul makeup remains aligned and true with what we present to the external world we will move in as realness with oneself and others. It is about being honestly yourself internally and externally as you move in the world with no guile or hypocrisy or superiority. This goodness moves us deeper into faithfulness.

Faithfulness is a trust element in a divine persuasion that we can have with God. We do not form it from other humans in the ideology of being confident. This faith in God is a gift to us from God to join God in an invitation and divine persuasion to trust God in all of God's wills and ways of our 'doing life' with God. Once we faithfully trust God's will and way of doing life with us, we are more likely to grow the fruit of the spirit of gentleness/meekness.

This divine fruit of the Spirit of **gentleness/meekness** is a self-control ability to become balanced in our emotion of expressed power. Some scholars speak to this in terms of anger versus righteous anger. Anger is a powerful emotion and if not bridled for the right time, place, circumstance, and purpose we could lose the credibility we seek in a situation. Using anger is for the greater good of another and/or charge and challenge them to see their darker fruits. Remember, an angry Jesus cleaning out a temple of cheaters and disrespecting dispositions in the house of God? This action of explosive anger was not Jesus' habit. He modeled a meekness of this fruit of the Holy Spirit in being balanced. Because to be in such self-control is the fruit of the Spirit that is the mastery of one's own self, but with the aid of the spirit. Without the Holy Spirit one cannot in their humanness alone master their own sense of self and doing life with a Holy God and with others.

Each of these fruits of the Spirit builds upon the previous one. We can grow nothing in the Spirit without the first fruit. The main fruit of the Spirit is love. "Whoever claims to love God yet hates a brother or sister is a liar. For whoever does not love their brother and sister, whom they have seen, cannot love God, whom they have not seen." (I John 4:20)

What would our Christian walk with God look like if we began the journey with a serious effort in the spiritual fruit of loving one another, as Christ modeled and taught? What would the dynamics of family life look like if we treated our own with an authentic love that showed respect and boundaries in our interchanges with one another? What would the congregational life of a community of faith look like that is bathed in the Spirit of God's love for a hurting world?

To claim a life of daily guidance with a Holy Three in One, the fruit of the spirit from Galatians 5 is a good compass to use through prayer.

What is prayer? Is it a wish list for what we want to have and have happen in our life? Is it a movement to mystery? Is it a practice that listening and discerning to something beyond ourselves? The meaning of the word to pray is to ask earnestly and please tell me your story.

God wants to have a relationship with humanity that has divine outcomes from the relationship. Thus, we have a God we cannot fully grasp and explain in a denominational box and claim all right answers and knowing about God. We must be honest that God is beyond us all who have striven to place something as holy as God into one faith, one denomination, and in some hierarchical element with human thumbprints declaring who God is to us.

Only God gets to say who God is in relationship to us in humankind. We only have the freewill to choose whether or not we want a relationship with God. Often our human limitations and lack of awareness's are projected onto God. It is from this projecting we often express who God is to us. We think we have captured God's holiness and essence of the Masterful Creator and then put that God in some boxes packed with our own ideology and own that God.

God told Moses in the Exodus story, "I am who I am and will be who I will be." This encounter reveals a God so holy that we are still ignorant to this day and time about who God is and is not. We know just enough from scripture to be awed and drawn and eager to know more for those who have eyes to see and ears to hear. But the 'I am' statement God makes is a statement of existence through all time. The Alpha and Omega: God is the beginning and end of all things. (Revelation 1:8; 21:6, 13.)

From the beginning, as God interacted with people in the biblical texts and stories, we see God reveal attributes of who God is and what it means to engage and relate to this God.

Anytime one wants an introduction into having a relationship with another person there is a need to get to know one another, build on this knowing so that each knows how to be with one another, and in being involved in a relationship then the doing of life together becomes a relationship that becomes tailored, defined, and blended into a relationship that has these attributes of knowing and being and doing life with one another. These relations are not just intimate ones from that of marriage. It requires these attributes in relationships between family members, friends, co-workers, colleagues, neighbors and even extended relatives.

But let us be real and clear; God is so holy that even typing and naming the holy names of God is to be honest about one's unholiness and unworthiness to even have a relationship with this God. It is God that wants to be alive and enlivened in our lives with God. The depth of love and generous One in creating out of chaos, voids, and nothingness is still the work of this God who offers us glimpses of who this Holy One is as the "I am who I am and will be."

Let us remember, God did not have to create humankind. God owes us nothing! God does not owe us an explanation about all our wanderings, whining, or wishes we cast on such a Holy One. God wants us to want a relationship of deep abiding love with Him. Any relationship that has authentic love and trust and loyalty and commitment will come freely out of our own freewill. The communication within these relating's will be enhanced on these attributes with communication.

What good is a genuine love and relationship within marriage, family, friendship, cordiality with neighbors, or progress with colleagues and coworkers without communication during daily encounters? These relating's would range from weak to non-existence without communication. The ability to love one another in all the complexities of loving would be futile without communication.

How long will any of these human relating's last if there is no communication?

What value would a friendship hold that never spoke to one another?

How loving and respected would a spouse feel if they never heard a kind word of gratitude or deeper sharing of your heart?

Where is the relationship of love when siblings compete and criticize rather than communicate?

Who wants to go to work and relate to coworkers who do not love with human kindness but rather with office politics and triangulations? Aren't our human-divine talents shared in healthy communication of fairness and transparency for the greater good of the company or business the best practices?

Where is the love through communication from a parent to a child or child to a parent who blames, shames, complains, and grumbles to bemoan and be right in their own eyes of false and faux pride? How healthy is a spiritual love between siblings when there is only constant competing and criticism?

When we treat one another this way in our communications, the relationships are devalued and devaluing of one another's human-divine personhood. If we will treat one another this way, then one must ask the harder question; is this the love we hold for God? Isn't the way we treat human beings in our lives indicative of our efforts to control how we view, love, and esteem a holy God?

So, when God invites us to know God more fully, be with God in our doing of our daily lives, then the communication standard of prayer needs to be rich with love. If the relationship with God is rich with love, then the joy will hold a maturing confidence that God's promises are real even in troublesome times. When the relationship with God has rested in these first two fruits of the spirit factors in the human-divine relationship, then even when life has its conflictual challenges, God's spirit will give you peace in that situation.

No matter the circumstances of life's celebrations or crisis or chaotic moments a relationship with God that is built on love, joy, and peace will be capable of forbearance and patience to endure a kind of suffering that may come our way, including the ability to be patient with the weaknesses of other believers and nonbelievers who stumble and fall short.

This allows for a spirit of kindness that offers benevolence to others and mercy, just as God shows mercy to you in your relationship. The character traits of spiritual fruit within love, joy, peace, forbearance/patience, kindness lends a goodness of seeking an upright heart of concern for another's wellbeing who may in most eyes not deserve it. It is at this crossroads to faithfulness and the ability to seek God's will and submit ourselves to God and ability to pray for our enemies as Jesus instructed in the Lord's Prayer. It is no small endeavor to be gentle of spirit and compassionate to those with shortcomings and fears that hinder their own wellbeing and often are their own worst enemy in spiritual wellness and harmony.

This faith and fruit of spirit traits marked and ingrained in our relationship with God, self/soul and others allows in the last element around self-control (meekness) to not become conformed to the world's standards but to live a life with God in the daily that reflects God's way of being in the world as one who loves, doesn't lose the joy and peace of God with them in times of trouble. One who can persevere, suffer, and be patient with the weaknesses of others. Press into concern for others with mercy from virtues like kindness, goodness, and faithfulness when encounters with others reveal fears that stumble themselves to their lesser selves.

Then comes the hardest one of all: is to have self-control over the costs that injustice has done, and they spill harms on the landscape of lives like a perfect storm leaves debris and devastation done. Forgiveness is possible with God's fruit of self-control within your own self/soul. It all began with love. God's kind of loving and nothing less will heal in the journey's course, where the fruit of God's spirit lives within you.

One of my beliefs about God is that God is all knowing and already knows my story and yours. So, in our conversing through the discipline of prayer, why does God need me to tell my concerns and details of my story? There is something spiritually therapeutic about hearing the soul spell out and spill out to God the details of a prayer that is often laden in petition, praise, worship, gratitude, seeking guidance, asking for care of others, and desiring to forgive and be forgiven. Paul tells us to pray without ceasing (I Thess. 5:17).

Jesus modeled a prayer life with God about having a dialogue, offering gratitude for food, going off alone to have long conversations with God, offering intercessory care of others, giving God praise and worship, praying for healing of others, discerning the will of God and lining up with God's will, praying for forgiveness of those who trespass against us and our own need for forgiveness. Jesus taught his disciples and us today that our attitude and posture in prayer is one of reverence, sitting, walking, standing, looking up, looking within, and observing beyond ourselves. Prayer conversations, reflections, meditations, pondering, are about being open to listening to God through the Holy Spirit.

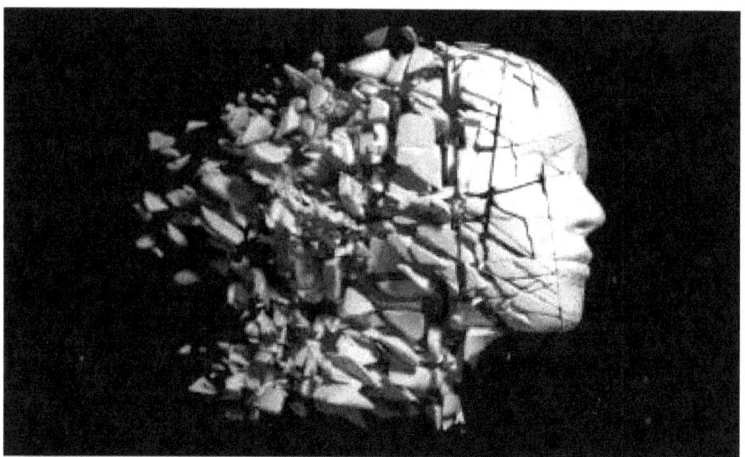

Fear

The bible offers us a vast number of commands bidding us to not fear and be not afraid warnings. After many of these fear warnings there is an encouragement reminding us that God is with us, there is good news and good tidings, or there is hope in any situation. The number one enemy to healthy love and loving relationships that are mature is fear.

We are often the culprit creating our own fears because of the choices we make, the lack of ownership we will face regarding our choices, or the reactions we have to those who project their fearful state onto us. There are also circumstances beyond our control that have fearful implications done to us too. In each encounter the task at hand becomes a way of facing the fear, addressing the fear, or fleeing from such.

Within the brain, we find the fear responses in the amygdala. We are naturally wired to use situations and circumstances with responses of fight, flee, or freeze. This area of the brain is where our emotions lie, and we manage fear through the way we manage our emotional response to a situation. When the amygdala has a hijacked disposition of hypersensitivity and over reactions to situations and circumstances that fear and fearfulness feed anxiety or phobias, then a person can become paralyzed in a state of fearfulness. Dr. Daniel Goldman coined this term, *amygdala hijacked*, from his studies on noticing those who are overwhelmed and overreactive to stimulus where fearfulness and anxiety are out of alignment with the actual circumstances being presented. The ability to manage emotions with resilience and reality is to grow one's own emotional intelligence into a healthier state is often more important to wellness in life than having a high IQ of mental intelligence.

The suggested ways and means to override a weakened and overreactive amygdala in the emotional center of the brain is to use more physical activity, prayer/mindfulness meditation, and address a reality check of the validity of the fear in question. This processing is helpful in overriding the emotionalism of the amygdala that may be over-exaggerating the responses one is having in each situation.

Money and fear will be the most addressed topics throughout scripture. God is fully aware of our wiring as human beings and these two topics are major factors in our lives that affect our ability to be at peace with God, Self/soul, and others by the way we handle our emotions and the impact of those emotions around fear and money. But we will look at money in another chapter.

For our purposes about fear it is vital that we are real and aware of how our emotions may fool us and rule us if we allow our emotions to be more in-control of our being in the world than is actually our authentic way of being in the world through a prayerful, physical, and purposeful vetting of those emotions.

Combine the characteristics of the Fruit of Spirit with that of this encouragement verse from second Timothy and we have a way of being in the world with God that is timeless in its challenging a healthy love, authentic power, and genuine self-control no matter the timeline of life we live on. Since the beginning when God created and joined humankind to see the image of divineness God offers us all to consider with him in relationship to him and we still to this day have the same choice the first humans had in the Garden of Eden story: Freewill to choose.

GOD

When God is at the center of our balancing a healthy love, power, and self-control along with attributes of the Fruit of the Spirit, we get a New Testament glimpse of God's desire from the beginning in the garden with the first humans. The story reminds us we would all fail and "fall short of the Glory of God", as Romans 3:23 says.

We can strive for this caliber of relationship with God, self/soul, and others but it will take the diligence of merging a Holy God and our freewill to grow up in the spiritual discipline of prayer, grasping the scriptures wisdom into our awareness, and self-awareness of our need to grow and nurture our soul.

Ask the Holy Spirit to help you find yourself in the stories of the scriptures. Imagine yourself being in the garden of Eden and you are one of the first humans in harmony with God and temptation comes, brokenness, regrets, blame, grief, hard work, toil, competition, lies that cost us our own wellbeing. Imagine the story of Noah's family, Tower of Babel, Abraham, Isaac, and Jacob. Imagine the challenges of Egypt, Moses, and the journey of being in the wilderness. Imagine the efforts and warnings of prophets like Isaiah, Jeremiah, Hosea, Amos, Jonah, and others. Imagine the New Testament God asking you and your young betrothed to take part in a human-divine birth.

Imagine being a disciple that witnesses and strives to explain the miracles, missions, and messages they experienced with Jesus. Imagine what it must have been like for Jesus to model the human-divine walk for us generation after generation to show humanity how to walk with this God that has striven to walk with humanity since the beginning.

Inviting us to listen, follow, avoid temptation, live life in the world but not of the world's mindsets: but to love the Lord God with all one's heart, mind, and soul. To give us holy lives over shallow versions of happiness through materialism and easy street with no bumps along the way because God is supposed to be a heavenly parent who serve us like a parent does a spoiled and undisciplined child.

Whatever our image and understanding of God is and our own inability to live in both gratitude and grief, death and life, wisdom and wonder, resilience and reliance, contentment and perseverance, determination and be still. When we live lives of expectations that God is here to serve our will as the created ones; we will miss the fear of the lord that is about respect and regard no matter the circumstances. We will be arrogant and treat God like it is God who owes us, and we know best. When we treat God this way, we will find it simplistic to treat others and another with the same lack of love, disrespect and disregard out of selfishness, naivetes, ignorance, unawareness, wantonness, and pride. What we will do to others, we will do to God. What we neglect and disregard of God we will also treat others likewise too.

Unhealthy pride is the gateway to the seven deadly sins that live with the dark fruits listed in Galatians 5, which directly opposes the good light the Holy Spirit of God is asking us to consider living our lives within a fallen and hurting world.

The seven deadly sins are lust, gluttony, greed, sloth, wrath, envy, and pride. There is much to be said about these layers of erosions to a healthy soul that loses their respectful fear and gratitude for God. The symptoms and outcomes of darker fruit character behaviors reveal not only what has been against God's best for us human-divine souls. But it (darker attitudes and actions from dark fruit) will clash and crash into the treatment of fellow human beings living out a life in the labels of Spouses, parents, siblings, children, women, men, environment, and animals.

Pride was the downfall of Lucifer and his followers against God. Selfishness of such an unhealthy pride is the gateway to the erosion of one's mind-body-spirit that costs their own holistic wellness and holy living with a living God. This unhealthy pride is the temptation to a slippery slope of all other marks made on the self/soul from our freewill choices that usually end in regret, anger, and deep losses with God, self/soul. And others. There is much to ponder on the angelic realm, heaven's hierarchy of beings and angels, and the details to the fall of Lucifer known as the morning star to become known as Satan the adversary. But that is another topic for another book. For our purposes, it is the fall of pride that we too must watch out for with our relationship to God- our own self/soul – and in encountering others.

God is more concern with our holiness of wholeness and wellness of our own soul/self with God, self/soul-awareness, and soul care of others than with riches, happiness, fairness, comfort, suffering, loss, and prestige. We will choose generation after generation and individual after individual from the Garden Tree of Knowledge of Good and Evil by our own freewill choices, just like the first humans.

Thus, the ability to live bold lives with God and die well on this side of heaven's realm depends on our freewill choices that will define us at the deepest tap root of our very being with God – Self/Soul – Others.

Before we can look at all the other compartmentalization of our lives, it would behoove us all to seek who is this God of all creation? What do we believe about this God? Do we seek this God and notice God in our daily movements of a day, a week, a month, a year, and so on? Do we compartmentalize God. Is God only found in a denomination, a few Holy Days on a calendar, some rituals and sacraments where when we participate in such it keeps us content about how good we are with God? But is God good with us in the 24/7 doing of life with a Holy One we call God?

How God was introduced to us is often how we will go forth and introduce God to others? There are moments when God was introduced well to a human-divine soul. Yet, God is rejected, or we add onto God character traits of the cultural updates of the times which make God's holiness enjoyable and user friendly to accommodate our own denials and sensitivities to ease our own consciouses.

I hope we will use these reflections, questions, scriptures, and compartmentalization's to self/soul-examine how we love a God of love.

If we love a God of love then how is that manifested in how we take care of our mind, body, spirit as we move in the world with God, in our own self/soul awareness, and with others we encounter or do life with?

Finishing Well

My husband and closer friends who know me are always hearing me speak to finishing well. The world is not fair. Life is both wicked and wonderful. There are positive and negative forces in this world that we all encounter and endure. Everyone is a walking story. Everyone must be honest about their own contributions to imperfections and perfections, positivity and negativity, sins and mistakes, regrets and no regret moments they have brought into this human-divine mix we call the human race. The complexity of the weeds and wildflowers that make us all up is part of the beauty of a God that still creates out of the chaos of us human beings.

None of us birthed ourselves into existence. God is generous enough to love us, and it is out of this love that he bothered to create us and this vast universe at all. That is the God I strive to worship with my life. If this read introduces you to the God Jesus pointed to and the Holy Spirit inspires us to notice in the daily, then these words of consideration and reflection will start the journey of living boldly and dying well.

If this starts a transformation of awareness that we all have one life that is in fact not compartmentalized, we will live bold lives worth living. We do such compartmentalizing for ease of control, and with an attempt at rationalization, explanation and often excuses around our limitations, our selfish expectations, and our lack of self/soul-examinations. The truth of the matter is this: **what we have is one wonderful life.**

It is through the lens of spiritual awareness of your image of God I invite you to move into the other chapters compartments of living out our lives. One of my own beliefs that the spiritual discipline of prayer has taken me is to see the spiritual being we are in our humanity.

So often we are human beings who occasionally sense that we have had a spiritual experience. We get back to our daily compartmentalized lives and neglect to notice a God that is with us, in us, for us, and wooing us to notice the spiritual being we are having a human experience.

What if the spiritual awareness enhanced and enlivened our human experiences were brought to these human encounters?

When we want to grow our knowledge, we read and learn. When we want firmer muscles and healthy bodies, we exercise and eat healthier. When we want to have a good connection with our spouse, family, and friends, we take the time to talk with them, do some life with them, and trust each other to have each other's back in hard times. So, why would we not need to know God, grow some spiritual muscles and maturity of resilience and gratitude, and finally actually talk and walk with God in prayer every day that includes listening and noticing God's movements?

Do you have access to dialogue with someone who is a spiritual director, pastoral counselor, ministers trained in discernment, therapist or trained social worker who values spiritual attributes of our human makeup? We are tasked in our spiritual awareness needs to seek wise counsel from others God's spirit will speak through and challenge us in self/soul awareness's. (Proverbs 19:20).

We will reflect our image of God in how we will treat ourselves and others. There is a direct correlation and revelation about how God will move in the world. God mostly invites and expects children of light who claim to be His to love one another with all authenticity. When we live this wellness in truth and authenticity of congruency we will finish well.

We know 1 Corinthians 13 as the love chapter in scriptures.

"If I speak in the tongues of men or of angels, but do not have love, I am only a resounding gong or a clanging cymbal. 2 If I have the gift of prophecy and can fathom all mysteries and all knowledge, and if I have a faith that can move mountains, but do not have love, I am nothing. 3 If I give all I possess to the poor and give over my body to hardship that I may boast, but do not have love, I gain nothing.

4 Love is patient, love is kind. It does not envy, it does not boast, it is not proud. 5 It does not dishonor others, it is not self-seeking, it is not easily angered, it keeps no record of wrongs. 6 Love does not delight in evil but rejoices with the truth. 7 It always protects, always trusts, always hopes, always perseveres.

8 Love never fails. But where there are prophecies, they will cease; where there are tongues, they will be stilled; where there is knowledge, it will pass away. 9 For we know in part and we prophesy in part, 10 but when completeness comes, what is in part disappears. 11 When I was a child, I talked like a child, I thought like a child, I reasoned like a child. When I became a man, I put the ways of childhood behind me. 12 For now we see only a reflection as in a mirror; then we shall see face to face. Now I know in part; then I shall know fully, even as I am fully known.

13 And now these three remain: faith, hope and love. But the greatest of these is love."

God with us in our stories

When my paternal grandmother was dying, I was with her. She had been introduced to a harsh Southern Baptist legalist angry God that sucked a lot of fun out of life and placed a high emphasis on work hard, put up with the inappropriate behaviors of others by turning the other cheek, stoicism and grace mixed with very little humor was her era of experience. She feared dying and hoped she was good enough up to the very end.

She was a proud woman from a Scots heritage. I held her hand and encouraged her by apologizing for the poor way in which she was introduced to God. God was far more grace filled and loving than this god of anger and rules around do not, and thou shall not legalism of Southern Baptist yelling and screaming preachers with congregations that followed suit. After some time of reframing this God as ready to welcome her with loving arms and nothing but grace and forgiveness, serenity, and peace, she relaxed and a few moments later she went without pain, fear, or signs of distress. She was peaceful, and her face reflected contentment and ease.

There is so much more to our story around family forgiveness needs, pride unchecked, sexism and egotism that feeds inequality in Southern family life and dreams unfulfilled because of the timeline of life she entered this world was not open to equality and options for women. Her soul had to grow, and faith had to persevere through resilience, forgiveness, and acceptance of reality. She could do this spiritual hard work from a place of love.

Every individual and generation, no matter the improvements or perceived advancements in technology and equitable living standards for all humankind; there is still the journey of choosing the fruit we will feed our own mind-body-spirit that affects our soul and relationship with God- self/soul- and others.

We will look at the consideration of our physical, emotional, vocational, social, cultural, and financial lives through the spiritual lens of a God that is for us and with us in each of these compartmentalization's that are simply our one wonderful life.

Ansel Adams: Yosemite Valley

Chapter Two

Physical

"Since our inner experiences comprise reproductions and combinations of sensory impressions, the concept of a soul without a body seems to be empty and devoid of meaning." Albert Einstein.

"Do you not know that your bodies are temples of the Holy Spirit, who is in you, whom you have received from God? You are not your own; you were bought at a price. Therefore, honor God with your bodies." 1 Cor. 6:19-20

"My flesh and my heart may fail, but God is the strength of my heart and my portion forever." Psalms 73:26.

There are plenty of statistics, authors, studies, and articles telling us about the cost of health care on failing ailing bodies and why. Likewise, there are a series of sources reminding us of the comparison traps we have over our body images and self-loathing if we are not the popular figure type of the present era's cover girls or model's aging well or not.

There are advertisers who strive to give us campaigns of genuine beauty comes in all shapes and sizes. Men and women compete on reality-based programs selling themselves in the outer shell of coolness, cuteness, cleverness, and charms while degrading themselves and others with words that roll off their tongues in ugly drama triangulations and tantrums. There is something sad and lacking if physical looks and classless character reveal the shells of humanity we have become and call it entertainment.

There are amazing feats and athletics that men and women show us, inspire us, and encourage us to find the athletic mover and shaker in ourselves. And we watch by the millions the Olympics in awe of the best in the world competing and pushing their bodies to the glory for the medal and sound of their country's anthem played in proud achievement for their team. We marvel at the sports ability of our favorite teams in every sport imaginable with every ball kicked, passed, hit, thrown, dunked, caught, spiked, dribbled, struck with a club, or putted in the hole.

Sport fans pay great deals of money and homage to these athletes in every sport with a ball in play. We spend substantial amounts of time and money to gain the talent to run, swim, skate, rock climb, weight lift, flip off parallel bar, balance on beams, ski downhill, and do extreme sports. We live vicariously through or admire those able to become Gladiators or American Ninja Warriors. Living vicariously, we delight at the efforts to push their body to great strength and nimble abilities to execute an obstacle course.

Beyond sports, there are the warriors of men and women who take their physical body to the max of survivor preparations for the military concerns around national security and safety of a nation and national affairs. These military personnel in all the armed forces go above and beyond physically for our countries demand for blood and treasure to defeat an enemy foreign or domestic that undermines constitutional freedoms and laws that defines a democratic republic.

Likewise, the first responders of police, firefighters, border patrols, port authorities, medic and medical personnel, chaplains and social workers hitting a crisis during their on-call duty and shifts that could go on for days before they go home to their own bed.

What about the body stretched and fatigued at giving birth, up all night, bottles, diapers, feedings, colic, and that is hard enough if attending to one little baby. New parents will physically push themselves like an athlete when several children have their own demands and needs of attention, hugs, and help in their little beginnings of helplessness.

Think of the car accident that mangled a body and cost the body a loss of limb, head injury, and handicapped parking spots are now a must. The illness and diagnosis that takes a body into decline, loss of independence, needs for assistance and help in body functions and care to the body they no longer can do for themselves.

Do we consider the body that is trafficked and misused by others sexually? The body of someone abused in a domestic violence, raped or sexually assaulted by someone they know? What of the body that is starving due to neglect, poverty, and eating disorders? And what about the body that has substance abuse concerns by medications, illicit drugs, and overuse of alcohol?

There are bodies that are loved well and cherished dearly in the vows of becoming one. The pleasure and intimacy that makes decades of being in each other's arms sacred nights that belong to no other but this one body.

There are bodies that are grateful for aging well and keeping their body in a healthy state of excellent vitals and keep living active and well into their aged days.

From birth to aged days, the movement and ability of the body is an amazing instrument of God. The events and challenges that take their toll on the body require some honest conversations about holistic care to one's body and the balance needed in self-care, soul and moral injury care for what we put the body through in this life.

In the first chapter on image of God and of our own spirituality of self/soul awareness, I offer the premise of noticing God in the routine, and events of your life. Now filter what your spiritual awareness and image of God in these scenarios around the various ways we use our bodies physically and the taxing this life's duties, demands, dangers, and destructions taken on the body by either our own doing or are done to us impacts how we experience God, self/soul awareness, and/or care or harm toward another's body.

How does God show up for the Veteran back from war and is wounded?

How do we sit with the love of God when the diagnosis is terminal, and the medical journey is torturous on the body?

How does God's love feed resilience, forgiveness, and compassion for others who have harmed another's body? On purpose or by accident?

How do we show gratitude and honor God for a good healthy body and appreciate it rather than compare and complain about what we dislike about our bodies?

How do we show gratitude and honor God despite a declining, aging body and appreciate it still rather than compare and complain about what we dislike about our bodies?

Our bodies are amazing! We are made in the image of God. Genesis 1:26-29 states this. "Then God said, 'Let us make humankind* in our image, according to our likeness; and let them have dominion over the fish of the sea, and over the birds of the air, and over the cattle, and over all the wild animals of the earth,* and over every creeping thing that creeps upon the earth.'27 So God created humankind* in his image, in the image of God he created them;* male and female he created them.28God blessed them, and God said to them, 'Be fruitful and multiply, and fill the earth and subdue it; and have dominion over the fish of the sea and over the birds of the air and over every living thing that moves upon the earth.'"

This Holy One in Three and Three in One existed in harmony together in the beginning. In Proverbs the eighth chapter is the place the Hebrew Rabbinic scholars remind us of the story of wisdom being born. In the Old Testament the Holy Spirit of Wisdom is feminine and in the Greek areas of the New Testament Jesus said that one greater than he would come into the world. This Holy Spirit is available to all who will hear and heed God's movement in the world through them filled with God's spirit. This Spirit is the advocate and helper known in the Greek of the New Testament as the Paraclete. This Spirit of Truth is the Spirit of God and desires to rest in the hearts of all who will allow the Spirit to enliven, discern, create, and live with God's will, self/soul awareness, and care of others. We are called to be salt and light in a hurting world. Listening, discerning, and joining the Holy Spirit's direction and care is our own prayer work.

Proverbs 8:23-33 "I was formed long ages ago, at the very beginning, when the world came to be.24 When there were no watery depths, I was given birth, when there were no springs overflowing with water; 25 before the mountains were settled in place, before the hills, I was given birth,26 before he made the world or its fields or any of the dust of the earth.27 I was there when he set the heavens in place, when he marked out the horizon on the face of the deep,28 when he established the clouds above and fixed securely the fountains of the deep,29 when he gave the sea its boundary so the waters would not overstep his command, and when he marked out the foundations of the earth.30 Then I was constantly at his side. I was filled with delight day after day, rejoicing always in his presence, 31 rejoicing in his whole world and delighting in mankind. 32 "Now then, my children, listen to me; blessed are those who keep my ways.33 Listen to my instruction and be wise; do not disregard it."

The book of Proverbs offers much wise advice on care to one's use of body, time, and affiliations with others.

Regard for the physical use and movement of our bodies is a part of spiritual wellbeing. Our bodies offer a variety of spiritual considerations in a world that offers us all the juxtaposition of chaos and confusion with that of awe and compassion. It is revealing and reflecting that the usage of our body is enduring, sacrificing, and offering us a mirror of ourselves in the encounters we have as we move in this world with our body.

Consider:

- So, God created man in his own image, in the image of God he created him; male and female, he created them. Gen. 1:27.
- I appeal to you therefore, brothers, by the mercies of God, to present your bodies as a living sacrifice, holy and acceptable to God, which is your spiritual worship. Rom. 12:1.
- And he said to his disciples, "Therefore I tell you, do not be anxious about your life, what you will eat, nor about your body, what you will put on. Luke 12:22.
- Do you not know that you are God's temple and that God's Spirit dwells in you? If anyone destroys God's temple, God will destroy him. For God's temple is holy, and you are that temple. 1 Cor. 3: 16-17.
- The eye is the lamp of the body. So, if your eye is healthy, your whole body will be full of light, but if your eye is bad, your whole body will be full of darkness. If then the light in you is darkness, how great is the darkness! Matt. 6: 22-23.

Our bodies are amazing! In the life cycle of cradle to grave the human body adapts and endures the growing, impacts, and systems complex intricacies done to us, by us or for us in the course of a day and in a lifetime.

However, a spiritual life with God can give us all the comfort, contentment, and an understanding that our bodies and physical care of our bodies matter. The decline, damage, and death of our bodies deserve some dignity too in how we address our physical health and care of our bodies too.

The aging process from some gerontology studies speak to decline of bodies, limitations and loss of independence are made easier to accept when there is room to tell a story. The defining of the body to what it can no longer do because of age, illness, or disabilities is to leave the human-spirit in isolation and depression for what is lost or gone. In our aging and declining physicality can we have gratitude for what was and what the body can still do that brings joy; like a hug from a loved one, a visit from a friend, and the presents of another in the room for human company.

Lovely Senorita

I had a patient once who had early onset of dementia in her sixties. She no longer gave eye contact; she had lost her ability to speak and cognitively make her needs known. The facility staff anticipated her needs for her with a schedule of routine bathing's, feedings, turning her and stimulation of talking to her. The only time I saw a response was when I would play the music her son told me was her favorite. She loved salsa music from her heritage. She would move her right foot to the beat of the music. Her skin was beautiful and had no wrinkles around her eyes or mouth. So lovely a face but with no expressions of pain or delight. But we all talked to her as if she were able to hear us around words since music was getting through to her. The human presence of others caring for her was not full of fear or fight. She was one of the gentlest souls locked in another world I had ever encountered. Her body was treated with dignity in this state of no self-determination from herself and her ease of people caring for her body was a spiritual example of do unto another as you would want done to you. (Mt. 7:12) Known as the Golden Rule.

The body from cradle to grave has so much to teach us about ourselves and one another not just physically; but emotionally and spiritually in our interconnected encounters with each other, with ourselves, and with God in the course of using, enjoying, accepting decline, addressing illness, absorbing mistreatment, adapting to limitations, or exploring the possibilities of what we can do with this one amazing miracle human-divine body.

It is vital that we accept the skin we are in for our own functioning in this world. Our skin covers our body as the largest organ we have. We come in a variety of human colors and every human color of skin is in the crayon box of life. Scientist tells us that as we shed our cells of skin, they become dust. However, our skin is the first line of protective defense for the internal protection of our body. Thus, cleanliness of our skin and protection from sun and environmental harms are vital to caring for our bodies. Scripture reminds us of dust, feeling like dust, and addressing the dust in our lives in over 100 verses.

In 1977 a new song written by Kerry Livgren of the rock band Kansas, released *'Dust in the Wind'*. The lyrics are haunting and resonate with the Book of Ecclesiastes chapter one. The sense that much of the world remains to march on another generation but the toil, the wind, the bodies of our work have a wandering meaninglessness to this life that returns to the dust we came from.

I close my eyes
Only for a moment, and the moment's gone
All my dreams
Pass before my eyes, a curiosity

Dust in the wind
All they are is dust in the wind

Same old song
Just a drop of water in an endless sea
All we do
Crumbles to the ground, though we refuse to see

Dust in the wind
All we are is dust in the wind
Oh

Now, don't hang on
Nothin' lasts forever but the earth and sky
It slips away
And all your money won't another minute buy

Dust in the wind
All we are is dust in the wind

The book of Ecclesiastes and the profound reminder of a 1977s rock band offers us the wisdom of reflection about our humanity 'under the sun'. While we are here, in our bodies and the skin we are in there is vanity and meaninglessness if we do not include God. It is from God we get our very breath for these bodies.

Our time can be brief at birth, shorten in youth, gone by middle age, make it to aged years, or last until being a centurion over 100. It is meaningless years, and our lives are dust if the Holy One is not a part of our acknowledgement as the author of our lives. The bodies and skin God gave us to operate from in the physical has deep spiritual ramifications for our own self/soul as we move in this world with the Holy One in wisdom as King Solomon finally concluded.

The timelessness of this message is our divinity with God lives for a short season in the humanity of here 'on earth'. How we live in these bodies shows God how much we respect God by respecting ourselves and others in each season of our lives with gratitude for the body and skin we function from while we are here.

Let the dust of our lives be a witness and worship of gratitude to God for bothering to give us life in these bodies.

The dragonfly is a symbol of transformation through wisdom.

The intricacy of transparent lace of wings, mobility, direction, and mechanics of a dragonfly are amazing. How much more amazing are we human-divine beings made in the image of God?

Creator God,

Give us wisdom rather than hooks of knowledge that snare. Let us see the order of breath, body, and skin as the vessel of talent, mission, and contribution we can bring as we co-create a life with you.

While we are here and before we are dust let us honor you with our mind-bodies-spirit. Let our lives have meaning because we are your children and the children of God heed wise use of our mind-body- and spirit. Amen.

Chapter Three

Emotional

"These are the ones who cause divisions, worldly minded, devoid of the Spirit." Jude 1: 19.

"But I say, walk by the Spirit, and you will not gratify the desires of the flesh. For the desires of the flesh are against the Spirit, and the desires of the Spirit are against the flesh, for these are opposed to each other, to keep you from doing the things you want to do. But if you are led by the Spirit, you are not under the law. Now the works of the flesh are evident: sexual immorality, impurity, sensuality, idolatry, sorcery, enmity, strife, jealousy, fits of anger, rivalries, dissensions, divisions. But the fruit of the Spirit is love, joy, peace, patience, kindness, goodness, faithfulness, gentleness, self-control; against such things there is no law." Galatians 5: 16-23.

"Emotions reveal what your heart loves and reflects your own self/soul." Dr. Deb.

I used children in the black and white photography depiction of emotions. Because, we do not even have to teach children to reveal their emotions. We have to train them to walk, eat, go to the bathroom, and eventually groom and dress themselves. But from the day they are born they have the ability to emote and express themselves.

With the physical body comes the intricacies of senses and emotional wirings of our persona. Emotions reveal us to ourselves and to others through our sense of right, wrong, wishes, desires, and can be rather a mess in the messaging. Our emotional intelligence or resilience, beliefs, and values uncover our emotional makeup of how we are seen and heard; likewise, how we experience others who reveal their emotional intelligence, resilience, beliefs, and values that are reflected from the emotional states they emit.

Beware of wolves in sheep's clothing!

There are those souls that have the ability to hide their emotions. There are some who have mastered using others emotions like strings on a puppet. Likewise, there are those who play on emotions to fulfill their agenda. Actors, musicians, politicians, news outlets, marketing, and commercial advertising has been pulling emotional strings on viewers and listeners for generations. These messages from such sources have their own power of influence to be vetted and challenged.

However, studies and departments in academia have shown us the dark misuse of emotions in narcissism, egotism, and anti-social disorders that impacts our own emotions. The DSM5 speaks to character and behavioral traits that include:

- Need to be impressive with a grandiosity pattern of importance.
- Expectation of being admired.
- Build up an idealized vision of the most important love, power, and success couple than others.
- Entitlement, special, and more unique than others.

- Displays a lack of empathy for others.
- They exploit others and use them with their charms, or they shun others that do not go along with the script of 'being admired', 'more important', or 'cross them or hold them accountable in any way.'
- Arrogant behavior with the only voice or opinion that matters.

What happens when we give no thought to how controlled we are by others? How do we go about vetting our own emotions and the impact of others playing on people's emotions? When we give up ownership of our own minds and owning the responsibility of our own self/soul's compass; then what? There continues to be a vast amount of work needed to explain the shifts and stats that speaks to narcissism and personality disorders. It is a prevalent study today in Western Culture.

Overt and covert narcissism are two common types. The overt one is more grandiose, manipulative of the narrative, and high need for importance or center of attention. The covert narcissist is more sensitive, self-effacing, and extremely sensitive to any form of criticism and having their pride shamed. Both types need to blame others and be honored for their successes and place in the organization, the family, the friendship, the marriage, and/or the community they are in. The covert narcissist is the most fragile of the narcissist spectrum and needs for all blame to be scapegoated on another or others through their need to be seen as the victim.

In religious organizations, a study shows that both types are significant in faith settings as clergy leaders. Both types will blame their staff, the congregation, or lay leaders of the church; taking no responsibility for the way they treat, shun, limit, or blame others for their shortcomings or leadership styles.

God may have given us all freewill and emotions to master; but evoking God and using titles of leadership to control entire sets of people for harm, control, and personal power is not faith, doesn't make for healthy families, and it is not of God.

Jim Jones

In my lifetime one of the hardest story, I followed in my young adult years was in the late 1970s. Journalists and politicians were getting wind of a young evangelist that began a communist-socialist commune of faith in Jonestown, Guyana located in Venezuela. Jim Jones was more cult leader and never a man of God, (Matthew 7:15) Jones used his honed charms and passionate enthusiasm to maneuver the emotions of those who were from the marginalized sectors of society and the seekers of that day looking for a utopian society. Like most cult leader types in their grandiose ego's and selfish agendas there is usually clues around misuse of sex, money, humiliation and control over others. All of which are red flags that are not the way of a Holy God. However, followers followed Jones from Indiana, to California, and later to the new promise land, The People's Temple in Guyana. There were over 900 followers of Jim Jones at the time of this horrible event in 1978 that came to a head.

Family members back in the United States began to ring the alarm of losing their children to this way of life without their parental permission, issues around money, and what was being preached by Jim Jones that sounded more cult than faith. This led to the climax of paranoia and control from Jones when Congressman Leo Ryan, fellow travelers with him and the press were shot and killed when striving to leave with the few congregants that also wanted to return to the United States. The few survivors of that day recount the complexity of this situation and the good people who were duped and controlled by a narcissistic leader.

Today, we use the slang term 'drank the Kool-Aid' as a casual reference to people who have no mind or thought of their own but merely the group think stance of what a leader or group tell others how 'it will be' if they are to be in sync with the leader. This term of slang came from this event where Jones had large vats of a drink made up laced with cyanide. This madness turned into the largest mass murder/suicide catastrophe involving United States citizens in 1978. Such a terrible chapter in our American story. This was the largest number of deaths in a single event until September 11, 2001 and the Twin Towers were attacked.

Sadly, history has been littered with stories such as this one. When we look to one human being or even a small group who do our thinking, living, and demand dying outcomes for the larger group listening to them; then there is a problem, and it is not of a Holy God.

Narcissism and egotism don't mix well for healthy outcomes in dating, marital, and family dynamic storylines and patterns either. The culprit is usually fear, shame, and unhealthy pride that makes up the hollow spaces that makeup a narcissist. They are like a wonderful rich chocolate bunny wrapped in gold foil. Presentation is good, the surface experience is enjoyable, and their charming words melt your heart. But, push, challenge, or require more from them of substance and they crack and reveal how shallow and empty they actually are inside with the wrath, blame, excuses, shunning, and shaming they do to fix the story of their greatness, while another or others are to be thrown away.

The key is to look for consistency, authenticity, and congruency of those fruit of the Spirit traits we have address in the first chapter on Christian Spirituality. The common thread to healthy relating's in any system or between individuals will show up with a foundation built on respect, mutual rapport, empathy, and concern for the greater good of a whole. An overt or covert narcissist will only look out for themselves and blame others.

Own your own emotions and prayerfully vet them with the Holy Spirit.

Scripture encourages we bring our emotions and concerns to God in prayer. To aid in lessening egotism that feeds into the even darker layers of narcissism is usually around fear and unhealthy pride.

Fear is addressed hundreds of times in both Old and New Testament. Fear not, be not afraid, do not fear are the arrangements of many warnings in scripture that remind us all that fear is an emotion that God wants to help us put in its place.

But just think about the previous chapter around the body of physical experiences. How does one not be afraid when they feel inadequate, get a bad diagnosis, experience an accident, bravely go to war and come back broken, show up as a first responder and shot in the line of duty, ran into danger and came back tortured by the memories, or have a healthy baby and the birth became a NICU– Neonatal Intensive Care Unit story or did not get to bring a baby home? How do we face losses emotionally and grieve those losses? How can a person not be afraid in the face of rejection, betrayal, false witnessing, and then treated with disdain by the gossip and opines of others' ignorant opinions? Would you not be afraid in a circumstance of injustice, unfairness, and mean spiritedness experiences?

In today's society, the use of social media has been a technology entity which unleashes a myriad of emotional ranges expressed, influenced and cancel culture, censuring the voices of some and highlighting the voices of others in approval of group think.

What if emotions run shallow, flimsy, and weak within us so we live a life of victimhood, depending on the opines of others, tallying the likes and hearts on Facebook for emotional self-worth? What if we withhold love and respect from family members unless you fit their lockstep expectations? What if our emotional wellbeing lived on the messages of commercials and cultures inputs? And what if social media manipulated our emotional maturity?

How do we master emotions, live with emotions that are often reactive and responsive to external circumstances and individuals who test our emotional boundaries? There are moments where events test emotional boundaries to the limits and make forgiveness a spiritual gauntlet.

2 Timothy 1:7 - For God hath not given us the spirit of fear; but of power, and of love, and of a sound mind (or self-discipline or control in some translations) To eradicate fear is to be of good courage,

brave, resilient, determined, and trusting that God's Spirit will give us strength and many of these attributes in the face of fear and fearsome encounters.

This verse has become one of my favorite New Testament verses. I came across it after my son returned from a camp event from his youth group and shared it with me. This was right before I went into seminary in my middle forties. This verse became a mantra for me, given how long it had been since I was in school writing papers. They challenged me to write dozens of thirty plus pages of theological papers and pass Hebrew and Greek. It was an overwhelming feeling for me. Sometimes the excitement of a dream coming true can show up and rattle the bones of fearing failure, being good enough, fitting in with classmates just a few years older than my own children, and hoping I am not a disappointment to my children and husband as I clamor to hold the schedule and demands of home, work, and school in smooth order.

I put these fears to rest as the circumstances of that season revealed the rest of that verse in actions and encounters unearthed around love, power, and self-control. Nothing reveals the motives and expectations of others more than the subject of love, power, and self-control. Since graduating in 2005 I appreciate and accept who is for me and who is not as I have navigated ministry, chaplaincy, family dynamics, and denominational faith leaders. There has been so much joy in learning as 'iron sharpens iron'. (Proverbs 27:17) 'Whoever would foster love covers over an offense, but whoever repeats the matter separates close friends. (Proverbs 17:9)

Growing the spiritual muscle of emotional intelligence and resilience erodes naivete and puts value clarification and ethics into perspectives that one can live anchored and sure-footed in uncertainty. Meditation on scriptures like 2 Timothy 1:7 and awareness of psychology age stage awareness growths gives me a foundation of wisdom and awareness around navigation of my emotions; but the spectrum from which another is using their emotional wellness or lack of wellness is made known too. The messy moments in responding and relating to one another have so many revelations around self/soul awareness that explains the God one knows or not, themselves, and others through the reactions and responses made, or not made. And there is much to expound upon regarding silence.

Emotional responses to life's shifts, experiences, and changes are revelation opportunities. When challenging times come into our lives, we are reflections of exactly what we are made of internally. People are like sponges drowned in a bucket of water. Let the events of our lives come up dripping, leaking, and pouring out of themselves once squeezed and pressured. It is in those moments the real elements and attributes of patience, empathy, resilience, maturity, gratitude, honesty, bravery, fears, malice, jealousy, anger, apathy, disregard, and a plethora of characteristic demeanors come forth out of ourselves and others to expose the uniquely and wonderfully made us that is lacking, growing, or wisely moving in the shifts, experiences, and changes we are going through.

Temperament and persona can contribute to how we express our emotions and present ourselves to one another under pressure. The healthier we are spiritually within ourselves however will also come forth under life's pressures, losses, and challenges. In a repeated examination of the verse II Tim. 1:7 notice that love is not an emotion it is a catalyst of action or lack of action that reveals a person's state of being who they are inside their very self/soul state. Power is used well or misused exposing the emotional state of being of a person's character. Emotions are often telltale signs of marker points showing us who a person is as we encounter and receive their emotional states of being or lack of emotional investment into themselves or another.

Jesus offers a warning and wise observation around noticing the actions of a person. All people have emotions but not everyone shows their emotions the same. Not all persons are equal in mature use of their emotions or are self-aware enough to master their emotions. It takes discernment and listening to the Holy Spirit of Wisdom to grow and nurture emotions that are intentional about utilizing healthy love, power, and self-control /discipline to be authentic and genuine in their human-divine growth. Many wear masks over their emotions as stoicism, elitism, intellectualism to hide the incongruences and hypocrisies of duplicities that rest inside themselves.

We have all fallen short of God's glory and there is no perfection in any of us human beings. However, there is a calling out of God's children of light to be salt and light metaphorically in a hurting world.

If we take our cues from the teachings and promptings by the Spirit, we find that our uniquely and wonderfully made self/soul will rise to our emotions being honed and healed by the Spirit within ourselves. The Spirit led Jesus to see John for Baptism and then the wilderness for testing his mission and message as God's Son. (Matt. 4:1)

This is an important modeling for Christian spirituality. Many scholars speak to the fact that Jesus was sinless, the Son of God, and the coming fulfillment of Isaiah's Messiah prophecy. Jesus will show human humility in a rite that will become a sacramental vow to be known as one of God's own. It marks this event in the Gospels as a sign with a supernatural break into natural order. The witnesses that remark a heavenly voice spoke, and a dove descended to acknowledge who Jesus was as John performed a rite, he himself did not feel worthy of doing.

However, John brought his own emotion of commitment and loyalty to God's calling on his own life as he joins in the ushering of a historical and spiritual marriage of human beings being joined to God by baptisms sacramental rites. Moving forward from this moment, the followers of Jesus as Rabbi will become something the world had not seen before that moment.

God willing to be fully human and fully divine and showing us in all humanity from every tribe, tongue, and temperament how to embrace our own humanity and divinity as we move with the Spirit in this world too.

There has often been a lot of emphasis on Baptism being about the removal of our sin symbolically and the new person rising out of the water of full immersion to become known as a new soul/self in Christ. To be candid and transparent, this author is not about to state emphatically that the only right ritual for baptism is full immersion, nor debate the various translations of scripture and theologies. Dogma and doctrine are not the highlights or dominate subjects in this spirituality conversation. What it highlights are the spiritual lessons we can learn about living a spiritual life in Christian Spirituality by inviting the Spirit of God's Holy Wisdom into our whole one life and notice how the Spirit manifests in the parts we human beings compartmentalize. Let us stay on task with the purpose of this short but deep pondering of a read in Christian Spirituality as a whole and holy way to live bold lives.

Daily habits make for holy habits.

In emotions and emotionalism attributes of oneself/soul the Spirit of Holy Wisdom is a discerning source which is available, again within our own freewill, to be activated in our life to assist us in the awareness of our emotion's strengths and weaknesses. Through the effort of prayer, scripture studies, and authentic ongoing self/soul examinations of motives in our emotions, we can grow spiritually sound and strong in faith, more mature in emotional intelligence, and soundness in emotional motives of congruency. This congruency comes from our ability to ask God to let the Holy Spirit examine our hearts, mind, and soul for those places within we would not let outward and what is put forth outwardly is not matching up with what is within us.

But, with God's Spirit of Wisdom, we can find a compass or plumb line internal and external dispositions and demeanors are authentic, genuine, and real as we walk in a world that has a lot of phony and fake facades.

This freedom of being real, authentic, and mature in the emotional intelligence of our own self/soul will offer us less posturing and posing that only feeds a hypocrisy in our own human-divine walk with God. To live with the Holy Spirit guiding and discerning our emotions into authenticity will allow us to take off the masks of piety, purity, and popularity from a source of superficial and surface level emotions of a feel-good faith, legalistic faith, or we got it all right and others are all wrong kind of faith.

I challenge us to face ourselves with the Holy Spirit's help. Our emotional lives can take us all over the rabbit trails of crazy making, judgmentalism, group think that stinks, and shallow living of seeking one thrill or hit from an emotional roller coaster ride after another. Emotions can warn us, free us, teach us, lie to us, get us into trouble, or empower us. But, without the Holy Spirit of discernment in serious prayer, we can fool ourselves into our emotions, and becoming our own thermometer reading of self-righteousness or live-in denial.

When Jesus finished with the rite of Baptism and God confirmed the status of who Jesus was to the witnesses of that day, the Holy Spirit of God led Jesus to the wilderness to be tempted. Why?

The reason is the simple fact that Jesus is our human-divine framework of how to live a human-divine whole and holy life. A preacher once said, "God is not interested in our happiness. A Holy God is interested in our freewill to live holy lives."

Temptation begins from an outside pressure to either ruin the good within another or expose the dark within us is stronger and easily provoked to come forth. The temptation in the Garden of Eden to the first humans was the enticing to be like God. Eat of this fruit and the knowledge of both good and evil defining's will be yours too; just like God, the Creator of you!

Jesus in the wilderness after a very long time of fasting and prayer is confronted by the Tempter to rationalize, excuse, explain away, and denounce a God that has more for our soul care than immediate gratification comfort of food, or the ego soothing's of prestige, power, and prominence of superiority over others. The Gospel of Mathew, Mark and Luke address this event from their various lenses.

It is Hebrews 2:17 that offers the why. "For this reason, he had to be made like them, fully human in every way, in order that he might become a merciful and faithful high priest in service to God, and that he might make atonement for the sins of the people."

Emotional lives exhibited and exposed by outside pressures, temptations, and situations that have not changed in procedures since the beginning of human beings striving to be like God, usurp God, blame God, and challenge God to do their biddings, on their terms, and their way repeatedly in every generation since the beginning.

In Jesus, it shows us we have a choice still to be spiritual beings having a human experience like Jesus and choose God's way of being human beings who are whole and holy in their spiritual-human movement in the world. It is not difficult to be human mostly and occasionally have a spiritual experience. It is not difficult to be human and deny all faiths with no deity acknowledged and simply do whatever your human heart desire on your terms every day. It is not difficult to look out for number one and be selfish in all relating's. There is no challenge to being human only. However, when we acknowledge our humanity is made in the image of God as Genesis tells us; then we have to pay attention to our humanity has a spiritual divine element in the mix of us and we are responsible in our freewill to choose. How will we move in the world with God-Self/Soul-Others?

Pick your fruit.

And we will know such by one's fruit that comes forth and out of them. Emotions are the mirrors of reflection that reveal the motives, character, and ethics a self/soul lives by as they move in the world. Emotions are opportunities to stop and reexamine ourselves for truth, freedom markers, grace, mercy, forgiveness, soundness, and sacred dedication.

A spiritual self/soul goes through the human experience of their lives and the sum of a life lived will either grow their spiritual wellbeing in the fruit of the Spirit, live an average to mediocre life of some spiritual growth or will not grow spiritually at all. Every generation chooses from the catalysts of their choices how they will grow their own spiritual wellness and wellbeing of their soul/self. Emotions play the role of actions, reactions, and passions from which growth is clear or not clear that growth is happening or no longer possible to grow spiritually given the choices we make from our own freewill.

Sadly, many Christians see their own spirituality as salvation is decided at the Baptism. This action means they have given their soul/self to God. Their ticket to heaven is secured, and the external sacramental rite offers little to show us of their fruit of internal growth spiritually. Truthfully, this rite is only the beginning of a lifelong eternal journey to grow one's soul/self in the way their own human-divine spirituality will move, grow, and become more of what God knows we can become.

There is a temptation to settle for our faith to be an emotional one filled with feel good feelings, content with a church community of fellowship, and enough emotional driven charity to check off our box of goodness to ease our spirituality into a lull of adequacy. Not that any of these outcomes are not good positive outflows of growth and do not offer us a solid faith in life. They do and these have merit to informing us spiritually.

The temptation is in complacency of not inviting the Holy Spirit to help you vet, in the internal self/soul of you, to notice if spiritual growth is taking place within. Is the internal you congruent with the external you? In every label you and I wear can other's sense from your emotionalism the state of wellbeing spiritually being ripened, offered, or barren fruit? How we respond and react from our emotions will give us a clue to how congruent and content we truly are with God, self/soul, and encounters with another self/soul. And noticing those reactions and responses will give us a clue in knowing them by their fruit and how that sharpens our own emotional awareness into spiritual awareness of our own self/soul growth needs. We need each other to sharpen our self/soul in growth and awareness.

Jesus at Baptism and the Temptation story only began the conversation of what it takes to become a spiritual being having a human experience. The human experience is the chance to deepen and grow our spiritual muscles too, as we sojourn in the wilderness of our human lives with the Holy Spirit as Jesus modeled in the wilderness story. It takes both the human experiences and the spiritual awareness's and experiences to hone us into the unique and wonderfully made human-divine self/soul God knows us to be.

We spent some time in this read to consider how we see God and what our understandings of this God is that we say we know. Now take some time to pray about your own self/soul authenticity of who you are and whose you are. How does God experience and see you in your fuller self/soul?

Prayer is the spiritual tool and conduit we use routinely and ongoing to be guided by the Holy Spirit as we examine and face ourselves, grow ourselves, and move ourselves to become the uniquely wonderfully made self/soul God sees we can become with the Holy Spirit's help. This is exciting stuff!

- Now the Lord is the Spirit, and where the Spirit of the Lord is, there is freedom. 2 Corinthians 3:17.
- May the God of hope fill you with all joy and peace as you trust in him, so that you may overflow with hope by the power of the Holy Spirit. Romans 15:13.
- But the Advocate, the Holy Spirit, whom the Father will send in my name, will teach you all things and will remind you of everything I have said to you. John 14:26.
- But you, dear friends, by building yourselves up in your most holy faith and praying in the Holy Spirit, keep yourselves in God's love as you wait for the mercy of our Lord Jesus Christ to bring you to eternal life. Jude 1:20-21.

And in Numbers 11 there is a wonderful story of Moses' exhaustion of leading millions of Israelites across a wilderness into a promised land that God would show Moses. The Spirit of the Lord in Old Testament was placed on one or two or a few; but not all, as Pentecost shows us by the New Testament.

Moses in his day wishes for such an event and in his need to have some leadership help and prophesy of support in leading the masses, God listens to Moses and tells Moses to bring 70 men that Moses chooses. God's Spirit delivered an anointing of the Holy Spirit and there were 68 men who prophesied and then knew their role of leading and assisting Moses. Two were supposed to be counted among the 70, but Eldad and Medad had the spirit of the Lord hit them later in camp and they prophesied too. Joshua was next in line to lead the people after Moses. He objected to their interruption and distress to the camp as something that could undermine Moses' authority as the principal leader.

Consider the emotional darker fruit of jealousy, pride, power, undermining another could be a part of what was seeping out of Joshua as he worried about Moses' loss of authority in the present could cost him his in the future. The response of Moses is one of humility, appreciation, and even hope that one day God would see fit to offer another Pentecost type of spirit dispensed to believers in the One true God. That way of following God through Christ and discerning work of the Holy Spirit would not come until Acts chapter 2 when the 50 days passed the Passover/Crucifixion took place a new Pentecost began in the Christian followers of Christ when the Holy Spirit came down as Jesus promised and the Spirit of God is offered to everyone and everywhere who believe in God. God is no longer relegated to one culture, a few Rabbis or Priests or Preachers. The Spirit of God is now available, as Moses would have liked in Numbers 11 in his dialogue with Joshua. God's Spirit will rest in all of us who will say yes to the indwelling Spirit of God.

But let us notice in the usage of this story the emotional maturity of Moses. The Spirit of God within Moses had to be aware of the settled places within Moses that he had no desire for power for the sake of power alone. Moses did not need to be in charge for his own ego of self-importance. Moses reveals his emotional intelligence of higher functioning by loving the people he led enough to ask for more help from God before the leading took more out of him than he had to give. A weary and tired Moses was wise too. He argued his case before God in prayer in chapter 11 of Numbers.

Seeking wisdom in prayer with the Holy Spirit of God is what Jesus modeled in his wilderness temptation to carrying his calling forward and fulfilling of God's promises and Moses in his directives of leading a people to a new life with God's promises somewhere else too.

A leader of faith continuously seeks the guidance of God through the Holy Spirit.

A person of faith continuously seeks the guidance of God through the Holy Spirit.

The fruit of them from within will bear this out!

Photo taken at a friend's cabin:

Elements of a sun, home, and hornets' nest. Symbols of balancing the harmony of heaven and hell moments. If we master such with the Holy Spirit, we just might find more heaven on earth than hell on earth. Thank you Holy One! Amen

Chapter Four

Social

"Be completely humble and gentle; be patient, bearing with one another in love. Make every effort to keep the unity of the Spirit through the bond of peace. There is one body and one Spirit, just as you were called to one hope when you were called; one Lord, one faith, one baptism; one God and Father of all, who is over all and through all and in all." Ephesians 4:2-6.

"This is what the Lord Almighty said: 'Administer true justice; show mercy and compassion to one another. Do not oppress the widow or the fatherless, the foreigner or the poor. Do not plot evil against each other." Zechariah 7:9-10.

"Social circles, groupthink, and generational mindsets offer us a foundation of positive and negative contributions to our thinking. How we think will affect our values, character, beliefs, and ethics from which an individual will strengthen or devolve. Love God with all your heart, mind, and soul and watch out for forces and sources that warp or whittle away your soul care and God's best for your spiritual wellbeing." Dr. Deb

Social wellness includes the ability to interact well with a variety of people through good social skills of communication, adapt well in a variety of settings and social interactions comfortably. Social skills and flexibility to interact well include the social strengths learned and encouraged within our own families. Social wellbeing is about how we interact and relate in our relationships with others.

William Turner in the mid-1500s was a physician, scientist, philosopher, and devoted reformations preacher. He is the source in the writing of *The Huntyng and Fynding Out of the Romish Fox,* to be the one who reminded us to observe the adage that birds of a feather flock together.

He was a reformer of his day that challenged the minds of the day to value science, question the authority of corruption in church and state affairs, and take a firm look at who one will affiliate with says a lot about a person.

Motivational speakers in the Modern Era offer the same business and getting ahead advice. If you are the smartest person in your group, then your group is too small. If you want to be happy, healthy, and wealthy, then hang with those types of people. We reflect who we are by the choices and willingness of who we will hang out with and spend our time with reflects ourselves.

The social circle of friends, the family essence at the core, the habits we use, the attitudes we exhibit all influence the person we become. For the good, and for the bad, these influencers in our life are worth vetting.

If the social circle of negative influencers costs you your self-esteem and confidence, keeps you from your dreams, promotes ideologies that are contrary to God's Word, and does not allow you to grow into your best self/soul potential then an emotional intelligence, search of scripture, and honest self/soul examination is recommended. Rise up and beyond these circumstances or influencers from social sources that erode your soul care.

When the positive social circles of friends, family, colleagues, and encounters feed and nourishes your soul/self with the kind of love we defined in the chapter on Spirituality: First Things then there is positive influence at play. Remember real love is an action and spiritual core ethic that positive influencers in social circle layers would desire for one another and everyone; including you. These positive encounters invest in our self/soul by being encouraging, willing to challenge each other kindly and fairly. Positive influencers will build on the maturing of Spiritual fruit within us because they want us to succeed in our own being as we move in the world.

Spiritually, we are all invited by God's Spirit to use our power of positive influence. There were about 40 scriptures offered in one Google search for the power of positive influence. I Googled out of curiosity the same search for negative power of influence, and it revealed over 100 scriptures. This simple comparison warns us it is difficult to be a positive power of influence in a sea of humanity that offers more than double the impact of those who will offer a negative power of influence in our lives. Therefore, the power of prayer and seeking wisdom about one's associates, friends, and influencers is so vital to a healthy spiritual life is how we live a bold life that is more sure-footed as we move in a challenging world. "Whoever walks with the wise becomes wise, but the companion of fools will suffer harm." (Proverbs 13:20)

There is an allegory of the two wolves or the two dogs that seems to have appeared in its earliest telling from the 1960s by a Baptist preacher named John Bisagno, and retold by Billy Graham in his book, *The Holy Spirit: Activating God's Power in Your Life*. This same allegory has been used often in movie lines and devotionals of reflective thought and meditations. They challenge us to acknowledge that inside every human is a source and force symbolic like that of a wolf/dog. One is fierce, violent, angry, and destructive while the other is nurturing, protective, righteously angry, and high yielding and productive. The moral of the story is to own one's own choices of which animal within them they will feed.

This 1960s story is nothing more than an updated modern version of the Garden of Eden story. The bottom line is that it has given us humans the freewill gift from God to choose. The challenges within our freewill is that of owning what fruit we will eat will affect us emotionally and spiritually. And thus, what our choices will produce in our relationships, affiliations, associations, and interactions with others come from the very fruit we pick and feed our own soul within us all will produce what we will become. Jesus said, "You can identify them by their fruit, by the way they act. Can you pick grapes from thornbushes, or figs from thistles?" New living Translation from Matt. 7:16.

Carl Jung would speak of these dueling traits within human beings through the lens of beginning warring sources, "Lucifer was perhaps the one who best understood the Divine Will struggling to create a world and who carried out that will most faithfully. For, by rebelling against God, he became the active principle of a creation which opposed to God a counter-will of its own. Because God willed this, we are told in Genesis 3 that he gave humankind the power to will otherwise. Had God not done so, he would have created nothing but a machine, and then the incarnation and the redemption would never have come about. Nor would there have been any revelation of the Trinity, because everything would have remained One forever." God wants a relationship with those who would choose to be One with God's love and not have to be. Is that not the relationships with others we prefer too? We want to do life with the very people who want us in their life too. Are we in relationship with God because we desire such or want God to serve us on our terms in the relating?" (Carl Jung).

Harmony within our imperfection.

This one wonderful and wicked life we work with and live with is our own spiritual journey. We decide how we will grow or not grow our own soul/self. I challenge us to consider if our will and God's will be in harmony and accord. Within the social attributes and influences we align ourselves with; these social influencers will contribute to informing, reforming, and transforming our soul/self into the us we bring to others too. Let me be clear here. We are influenced by the positive and negative social influences while we are here on this timeline of our life journey; we too are both positive and negative social influence on others' soul/self's too. However, since we choose our responses and reactions to the positive and negative experiences encountered in social influencers, we get to decide how we will be and move in this world.

We cannot be our best, truest, freest, and highest self/soul without acknowledging that imperfection will always be within us. We can strive for our self/soul to be at our highest, best, authentic, truthful self/soul by utilizing the Spirit of God within us for Wisdom's sake to move in this world despite other's flaws and our own to rise and offer our best, anyway. Ephesians 4:23 invites us to let the Spirit renew our thoughts and attitudes.

With wise ways of interacting with others, it is the Book of Proverbs that has timeless lessons on navigating well in unholy moments with people who do not have your own best interest at heart, even if their slick ways and charming words say they do. Our lives are interconnected in every facet and compartmentalization this book will opine for offerings of living boldly and dying well with our own self/soul.

Through an active serious prayer life of vetting with the Spirit of Holy Wisdom we can all improve our odds of fewer snares, missing of marks, and getting hurt or harmed by the encounters of those who have agendas of selfishness, ignorance, arrogance, unhealthy pride, and immaturity that feeds so many ism's in this hurting world.

This world is a wonderful world. This world is a hurting world. This world is a wicked world. This world is a generous world. This world is a challenging world. This world is a fallen world. This world is an amazing world. This world is a beautiful world. This world is an ugly world. These domain descriptions of the world all hold grains of truth in describing this world full of human divine beings. We can hold all these descriptions and find truth in the statement.

The challenge for us all as spiritual beings having our human experiences is to ask a deeper question about our quest here in this world. If we all contribute to this world, our own self/souls as we encounter one another; then it begs the question of contribution from our freewill. Is the world a better place because we are here and in it from our best soul/self? What side of our soul/self do we feed the most and then give a dose to another? Do you see the gift of your own soul/self being lessened and/or enlivened within your social groups? Or are you having to accommodate some lower or erased self/soul version of yourself to fit into certain social sources?

Likewise, if we are human beings that have spiritual experiences, we have additional questions to explore in such a quest. Are we as intentional about growing our spiritual understandings as we are our human minds in intellectual academic understandings? Are we able to have eyes and ears open to notice God's movement in the world? Can we encounter the Spirit of God in the encounters of nature, a conversation, a line in a movie, from within ourselves as we pay attention in a 24/7 timeframe? Are we discerning through prayer and knowledge of God's will to distinguish the wisdom of the Holy Spirit from the spirits and influencers that hoodwink and mislead us?

It is worth repeating what I said in the beginning, "the social circle of friends, the family encounters you have, the habits we avail, the attitudes we exhibit all influence the person we become. For the good, and for the bad these influencers are what we should vet and reconsider if the influence is negative, costs you your self-esteem and confidence, keeps you from the dreams God has placed within you, and does not allow you to grow into your best self/soul potential."

Chapter Five

Cultural

"There is neither Jew nor Greek, there is neither slave nor free, there is no male and female, for you are all one in Christ Jesus." Gal. 3:28

"And he made from one man every nation of mankind to live on all the face of the earth, having determined allotted periods and the boundaries of their dwelling place, that they should seek God, in the hope that they might feel their way toward him and find him. Yet he is actually not far from each one of us," Acts 17: 26-27.

"Culture is the whole complex of distinctive spiritual, material, intellectual and emotional features that characterizes a society or a group. It includes creative expressions, community practices and material or built forms." from Our Creative Diversity: The UN World Commission on Culture and Development.

Cultures have an ethnic complexity of social, religious, political, historical, and traditional customs and shared experiences that offer a group identity. From one cultural group to another, there are similarities and differences that will influence who we are as a collective whole. There are modes of dress, beliefs in faith (s), unique cuisines, types of dance, celebrations of events around the calendar year, and customs to consider.

There was a culture centuries ago that left one land to go to another. They faced their oppressions, fought for their survival, had their ways of patriarchy and matriarchy standards of propriety. There were board games, cards games, and dice. There were religious rituals. Fathers taught their sons a trade starting at around age five. Mothers taught their daughters how to manage the business of running a home. Some tribes and clans could be as large as a small town, and it was no small thing to lead or protect their own. Servants and slaves were commonplace. Herdsmen and personal armies of protection were commonplace as well. Grinding their own wheat and grain into flour allowed for a main staple of bread.

Eighteen centuries later a family from this linage would have to go from place to place to avoid persecution and oppression, had their patriarchy and matriarchy standards of co-existence. There were board games, cards games, and dice. There were religious rituals. Fathers taught their sons a trade starting at around age five. Mothers taught their daughters how to manage the business of running a home. Some tribes were no longer in existence and groups of families could be large, but it was more village oriented than nomadic towns on the move. Servants and slaves were still commonplace for those who had means to provide for such staff of support. There was no informal or formal army of protection for the villagers. Grinding their own wheat and grain into flour allowed for a main staple of bread.

This simplistic snapshot of a group of people highlights the normality of life from Abraham to Jesus of Nazareth. Eighteen centuries apart and routine layers that describe a culture of people have changed extraordinarily little from generation to generation.

The inspiration is in the details of the stories in those eighteen centuries.

This slow progression of changes and traditional nuances that capture the essence of a culture is the same in all of humanity. All the identities of the earth come from a commonplace of beliefs, values, worship, food, dance, games, rites of passages, male/female roles and rules, work, oppressions, provisions, protections, and the making of bread.

The staple of bread goes all the way back into antiquity. Every single culture has a recipe and routine for making breads. The bread may be flatbreads, pita, pumpernickel, rye, wheat, multiple grains, biscuits, small rolls, leavened and yeast. Whatever the makeup of the bread, every single culture in humanity has the commonality of bread making as a staple to their heritage.

My heritage is Scots-Irish-English. These ancestors would have used soda and lard to get a quick rise into a loaf of bread or scones that had raisins and fruit bits in it for sweet bread. The Americanized version for our family became my paternal grandmother's homemade lard Southern biscuits. She was born in 1917. Three years before, women in America ever had the right to vote. Her generation of women were rarely educated past the eighth grade. There were long hours for running a farm and caring for family members of the very young to the very aged who came to die under her care.

Not much changed really in domestic family life in eighteen centuries of Jesus's lineage. There are wars, stories of loss and cultural shifts to move here or Exodus there, but the routine within the family structure of culture and even the staple of bread had very few changes. My grandmother's people came to America from Scotland around the late 1600s. From what I can tell from family culture to a Scottish-Irish American culture in the South; not much changed in those few centuries really either. The mornings when we all awoke to biscuits baking seemed timeless no matter the century that the experience of fresh baked bread waffling in the air offered.

Change is inevitable.

Yet today cultural nuances are blending with one another and eroding at the hems of history with something new and shifting into something else. In two and three generations the number of women in our American family of Scotts-Irish heritage have gone from middle and high school educations to a multitude of us with masters and doctorate level educations. What I am keenly aware of is the lack of bread baking from scratch that we do now in my family, and the many people I know from other cultures profess the same lack. Industry and automation have made it easier to buy any loaf, style or type of bread one would want from a local grocery store or bakery.

Just as families of a cultural heritage have their long history of subtle shifts and slow changes, so have the broader cultures of so many of us until now.

In Phyllis Tickle's book, *The Great Immergence: How Christianity is Changing and Why*, there is a historical thesis of awareness that major shifts in cultural ways of being take place around every 500 years. She proposes an observational awareness that the cultural trends and influences of our day are impacting, reacting, and a clarification of how the church remains relevant, strengthening, and resolute in the changing period of a major restructuring of culture.

What is not changing is the idea that Judeo-Christian and any other faith tradition is the leader of culture. It is not. Faith communities lead people to understand God in a changing world, notice the discernment and movement of the Holy One active in a changing world, and find their own growth and rhythm with the Holy One's Holy Spirit as they charter their own course in a changing, shifting set of circumstances in the world.

But Jesus told him, "No! The Scriptures say, 'People do not live by bread alone, but by every word that comes from the mouth of God.'" Mathew 4:4 This verse is part of the conversation between Jesus and the Satan or Evil One in the Temptation Wilderness story. This is relevant and timeless in a time of shifts and cultural changes which will have its effects on the church universal. No matter what denomination and tradition within Christianity we ascribe to the spirituality influence of the Holy Spirit does not change.

What changes is how we human beings acknowledge how little we actually know, experience, and are acquainted with the Holy Spirit of God. The trend in social media is to project our emotional feelings of warm fuzzies on a Jesus we see and feel through the influence of a soft and syrupy Jesus in contrast to the angry old man of God in the Old Testament. The beauty of moving songs of worship, tears of emotive gratitude with hands raised, or appreciation of God's Creation in nature to be environmentally protected is not the cultural clash or complaint to be made here. There is truth to this being a part of a cultural shift that has its positives. There is no one who can declare what is shallow or superficial or not shallow or superficial by an observing projection or opining opinion. God knows exactly the shallowness and superficiality of hearts in any generation of cultural routines and rites in the church, temple, and synagogue worlds from the start of time. So, let us agree to be honest with ourselves. While faith traditions and denominations all get some attributes of God right, they have all erred in time and put God in a box they own and been wrong too.

How has God changed?

Thus, a word of consideration in a world that has exploded with a love for Jesus and Spirituality that is growing in rich openness to the beauty of being alive in a fast-paced world; let us consider a slowdown and savor getting to know the God that sees you.

That differs from our vantage point of projection of what we think our own image of God is in the twenty-first century. If we are not careful in this fast-paced shifting of time around faiths, we will take a God of a few hundred ideologies around God and make God into our millions of ignorant versions of who God is to us. And like the denominations and multiple faiths there will be some who have it a little right and a lot may by wrong too for the next century of generations we introduce to a Holy One.

This is where the church can benefit culture. Our Spirituality may not always be from a religious organizational tradition. However, many religious traditions offer a rich spirituality that has been underutilized in the twentieth century culture. It would behoove faith traditions to educate the congregation of the spirituality that undergirds the image of God that was never introduced as the angry God of the Old Testament or the angry God who would kill his Son on a Cross. This introduction and stereotyping of a Holy One is so far off and we the created are ignorant of who this Creator God and Holy One in Three in the various Christianity faiths is about.

Most are too busy telling God how to be God in their prayers and what their laundry list of petitions are they have not recognized the arrogance of the ignorance of this approach because their image of God is skewed by cultural influences.

There is a lack of basic bible knowledge of getting to know God and notice God in the sacred writings from the context of Hebrew, Greek, and Arabic meanings within the text. We overlay our own cultural words and meanings onto God from the meanings of words from our own cultural understandings to make the God of our own understanding fit what makes us feel good about ourselves.

If you had a friend that was your friend from the perspective of only their opinion and projection onto you but not actually **know** you; how meaningful will that relationship be to both parties? I suspect shallow to mediocre or not at all would be the answer.

This is the danger of culture leading faith traditions, and this is the challenge of faith traditions in spiritually growing those souls from culture that come to learn and worship as community. There is a root from the start of time that must respect God's own words about God's own self as Creator of Humankind.

Every relationship with this Holy One can build on a personal God that knows them by name like the God of Abraham, God of Isaac, God of Jacob and so on down through time until it is your personal relationship with God.

But heed this root of warning no matter the generation or the cultural mindset; neither Abraham, Isaac, Jacob, nor any human created being gets to tell a Holy One how to be God of all of us ever, my friend. There is one hierarchy that will not change from the Alpha to Omega in any generation or any culture or growing shifts of mindsets: God is God, and no one tells God how to be God.

A fearful, respectful culture would be best suited and honoring to never forget the order of first things. All humankind are the created ones. We are indebted to the Creator One who never had to give us life but loved us generously enough to do so and continues to create and sojourn in the chaos of humankind's cultural ways and means.

Bread of life

The bread of life from Old Testament to New Testament gives us this literal and symbolic understanding in the utilization of bread as a source of life.

In Exodus 16:4 God let Moses know, "Behold, I am about to rain bread from heaven for you, and the people shall go out and gather a day's portion every day, that I may test them, whether they will walk in my law or not."

In the New Testament, Jesus speaks to our praying to God for our daily bread in Matthew 6:11 amid the Lord's Prayer. And in John 6:32-35 Jesus then said, "Truly, truly, I say to you, it was not Moses who gave you the bread from heaven, but my Father gives you the true bread from heaven. For the bread of God is he who comes down from heaven and gives life to the world." They said to him, "Sir, give us this bread always." Jesus said to them, "I am the bread of life; whoever comes to me shall not hunger, and whoever believes in me will not thirst."

There is much to unpack here in the spiritual provision and purpose of this symbolism and literalism of bread in our human-divine lives Jesus modeled and messaged for us to notice and invited us to follow.

Notice God wants a willing human divine soul to walk with Him in his ways and laws. In the Old Testament story of his conversing with Moses, we hear of God's love and provision. We are loved; we are provided for in food in supernatural ways that only God can offer and yet...... we are tested and invited to show our willingness to be in the relationship WITH God. Not robots and legalism, but freewill from our own hearts. In our human relationships we have our own versions of preferences, tests, expectations of the relating from freewill we want from others too.

What good is a relationship that has no sense of a want to, loyalty, and boundary expectations that offer mutual regard and respect for the relationship? So, why are we surprised that some of God's character traits in desiring our relationship with Him have some tests of trust, loyalty, respect, and freedom that is steeped in a loving invitation? Don't we want such attributes in our marriages, friendships, families, colleagues, and neighbors? Be honest!

What has changed in this invitation of bread provision and purpose with God of the Old Testament to New Testament? The value of Jesus. Now the bread of life is God's own Son being offered to live, love, and give of himself to the entire world. Without Jesus, this Holy One called God is left to one culture and a smattering of a few that join that culture.

Jesus is the bread of life that is the game changer of God, giving even more to God's own creation of human-divine souls. Jesus as the metaphorical and symbolic 'bread of life' in our daily bread of trust, love, hope, grace, forgiveness, loyalty, mercy and freedom offered to everyone who will say yes to God within this even deeper cost for loving us all!

Personal Cultural Influences

A Holy God went beyond one culture and invited all cultures to join in the relationship with Him. My ancestry would have come from Ireland and Scotland with a heavy dose of Celtic worship for nature and solstice seasons in those pagan roots of gratitude and appeasing many gods. Following our DNA in Ancestry lineage has grown in interests over the past decade with DNA analysis. My own rests heavily in Scots- Irish-English-Creek Indian and even some Viking from Scandinavian influences in about the 1500s, according to Ancestry. It is fascinating.

With sincerity and some humor, I am aware that the many cultures that roll through my DNA influence me at some spiritual thread that leads back to nature of Celtic ancestry in Ireland, Scotland, and England with heavy doses of love for trees, water, fire, and earthy grounded-ness to the land. It explains my love for seasons changes, the beauty of trees, greenery, and hearth of home in the holidays from before advent until after Epiphany. The sound of music from wood winds, bagpipes, Celtic harp and fiddle captures my ear and the words of a good ballad or story in song vibrates in my blood. The roots of our American country music come from these roots of storyteller songs utilizing a variety of string instruments, percussion, and flutes to capture the emotions of the song telling of something humorous, sad, love, or faith.

Yet, there was a time when these lands and people of my heritage were also pagan and ignorant of a One true God that made the trees, fire, stone, water, and earth for planting and feeding human and animals alike. This gritty existence was loaded with superstitions and multiple gods to appease for protection of fertility and production of provision for family and livestock.

St. Patrick is known for bringing the message of Christ and the One true God represented in the Trinity to the Irish. He had been a boy captured and pressed into slavery for the Irish. He escaped and returned to England where he went into the priesthood. In prayers one day he felt the Spirit of God asking him to forgive and take the message of Christianity to these Irish folks in the 5th Century. England and Scotland had heavy Christian influence from the occupation of Rome, Catholicism, Protestantism, Anglican and Monastic life imprints since the 4th and 5th century and Protestant Reformation and Anglican influences of the 16th century. Cultures morph and blend over time and Celtic and Protestant influences are prevalent in my ancestry. Each of us can look at the influences of histories military occupations, wars, famines, rulers, and a plethora of influences on specific timelines beliefs and values of a culture of then versus now.

From the beginning of the introduction of Christianity through Jesus, Disciples, Apostles, and Paul; there has been a variety of Jesus followers from cultures and cultural influences all over the entire globe.

The issues of change in culture and Christianity in multi-cultural settings has been changing, blending, and morphing not only in my heritage; but everyone's heritage and faith traditions origins have had cultural blending, influences, and shifts in their ways of faith. Subtle at times but changes, nonetheless.

Change from Jewish religious leader – Christian killer- to Missionary Establishing Christian Churches

There was a man named Saul who became known as Paul. Paul would do his missionary work and so would a vast number of disciples who went beyond Jerusalem's walls and Jewish cities to tell the Good News of Christ. Jesus told them to go to the end of the earth and invite all and dust of feet from those who say no and leave them in peace.

The backstory of Saul to Paul transforming into a Zealous Jesus follower began as a Zealous Rabbi who had Christians stoned, killed, and harassed by the hunting down efforts of Saul himself. There is an observation to be made here about this man. The same man who loved God so much as a Jewish Rabbi would address a cultural shift of Judaism that would include the Jesus' teaching and message of being sons and daughters of God as blasphemous. Jesus was not the Messiah messenger this culture of the day wanted. They wanted a warrior like King David and a ruler that made Roman rule get out of their homeland, beliefs, and expectations of being God's chosen people.

It is quite a miracle making moment of Saul becoming known as Paul. Think of the Holiness of God stepping into supernatural moments for Noah, Abraham, Haggar, Joshua, Daniel, Jonah, Mary, Martha, Joseph, Lazarus, and Jesus. These and more can show us a God that communicated, and people heard the covenant of commitment, went from barren to pregnant, needing the sun to stand still, the lions not interested in mayhem or dinner, the whale of belly or delivering to dry land, more miracle births, and raising from the dead.

When Saul comes along, he values the God of Moses that parted the Red Sea and saved his people in the Exodus from Egypt. In Acts 9 we find Saul is on his way to synagogues in Damascus from Jerusalem in what is just under a 1.5-to-2-mile walk. He and two companions are going to address the Christian movement known as 'The Way'. Verse five shows us an encounter takes place of light, voice of Jesus, and questioning Saul. "Saul Saul, why are you persecuting me?" Two witnesses heard the voice and watched Saul become blinded. They took him to Damascus and remained in a state of prayer and reflection on his experience as he remained blind for three days. Jesus, spoke to a Christian leader Ananias in Damascus to go and heal Saul with restored sight. The trust conversation begins about trusting Saul given what his reputation offers and trusting Jesus given he is the Way these new budding Jewish Christians are following.

This event, encounter, and evolution of awareness took Saul into a journey transformation of a cultural faith of Judaism of that particular day and move into a willingness to be missionary and Apostle Paul. As Paul, he went into three missionary journeys, suffered beatings, shipwrecks, jail, and positive establishments of seven churches and other communities throughout Asia Minor.

The miracle remains that in these days of shifts, changes, and cultures that Paul went to spread the Gospel; he stood in a variety of places far different than Jerusalem. Each church from Jerusalem to Corinth, to Galatia to Thessalonica, all had their own cultural nuances, beliefs, and values that impacted how they took in the

Christian message. From the beginning his letters were to challenge, instruct, and help the readers address the cultural surrounding that was not a Christ ethic for Christians, what was acceptable and what was not.

Paul's letters went to so many eyes and ears from a variety of cultures throughout Asia Minor. He had to exhort and encourage a consistent message of faith, behaviors and ethics of Christ versus the various cultural wars of his day. He also had to defend his name and his own right as Apostle and leader who suffered for the cause of Christ to be heard! Letters were his way of striving to cut through the unconsciousness, ignorance, power grabs, and false teachings attempting to infiltrate the churches.

Paul was in the thick of cultural wars of societies throughout Asia Minor as a man of zeal for God. As a Jewish leader in the Pharisee sect of Judaism where they believed in a resurrection afterlife. And in this life, one must follow the laws of Moses and the many laws that the Pharisees taught the Jewish people to live by in their daily lives as they interpreted the Ten Commandments and Torah. The Pharisees had over six hundred additional commandments of law-abiding ways to live to be a good Jew. They comprised of both positive and negative warnings built off the Torah, known as good ways of being (Mitzvot aseh) and what a person must abstain from that is negative influences (Mitzvot taaseh).

Thus, this is important to note on the background of Paul because his transformation from this way of living for God was radically changed when he encountered an experience with Christ on the Damascus road. As a learned man of the Pharisees sect in early Judaism he was huge on living a strict life and killed Christians as blasphemers as an act of honoring God. Freedom in Christ and having a personal relationship with God through Christ was radical teachings to be sure.

In Paul's conversion, missionary trips, sufferings, imprisonments, shipwrecks, and challenging the culture wars of his day was no small task for furthering the messages of how to live as a Christian in the variety and diversity of settings he traveled. But Paul was wired for and gifted in knowing exactly what laws of living were of God from Christ's teachings and what was cultural that tripped people up into legalism in a religion rather than a living out of faith with God because of Christ and God's Holy Spirit.

In Paul's day there were dietary issues, circumcision, and Sabbath laws that were intense. A man could get his ox out of a ditch or rescue a sheep in his flock on the Sabbath but not work or heal humans on the Sabbath. (Luke 13:16) Jesus challenged this belief while he was alive and now Paul does in his letters and travels. The irony of being one of those who debated and added to such legalism of living is now the ambassador for Christ in mercy, freedom, while honoring the Ten Commandments and the Beatitudes of Christ. Paul offers this awareness in his letters to the churches to Gentiles and Jews alike as he went about his missionary work.

Can you imagine with some empathy and ability to put yourself in the efforts of Paul who strove to reason with some unreasonable mindsets and circumstances of his day? How would you sit in house churches and beginning efforts to learn about a faith of freedom and commitment to Christ in a time that would kill you for being a believer or limit your livelihood for being a believer? The churches of Ephesus and Corinth were steep in cultural habits and ideologies that were not godly for a Holy God. The new followers of this Jesus were called Christian's approximately fifteen years after the Crucifixion of Christ and it was a slur not a compliment.

The squabbles and tug of war in Paul's day was simply the beginning. James and Peter have the same debates over dietary and circumcision expectations on Gentiles in Jerusalem and other places in order to be this follower of a Jewish Jesus. The culture of churches in Paul's day had to wrestle with what is sacred, secular, and influencing the Way of Christianity. That has not changed down through the ages.

In my own ancestry of Scots-Irish is a culture of Celtics who worshipped nature, solstice days, multiple gods, and an afterlife hierarchy system. Christianizing the Celts would have been a different Christian community than the ones Paul addressed in Greek, Roman, and Jewish cultures. The essence of the Gospel's transcends cultures and also makes room for the complexity of cultural diversity in the journey of Christianity shifting and changing with issues of these days.

As the broader world heard the Good News and Christianity moved into cultures like Germans and Celts who valued winter solstice and trees; the Christmas tree became a part of the Christian celebrations influenced by culture and culture influenced by Christianity. In the early church the shift from no pork and no circumcisions were no longer a law of the faith requirements. People could be deep persons of faith and eat pork in their diet and Gentiles of the day were not required to be circumcised males in order to be considered a person of faith in this new Jewish Christianity of Paul's day that moved into the whole world and all cultures.

Jesus takes us into the hospitality of welcoming us to join in on knowing the One true God that Created the seasons and all of nature. To live with God's movement in the world through the Christian following of Jesus, and discernment of the Holy Spirit offers us a diversity in Christianity that includes us, them, and them, and them, and them and everyone in every single culture from every corner of the globe. That is a God of tough and tender Love. This is the Holy One in Three and Three in One that I am eternally grateful for being included into God's family beyond the cultural nuances of any culture. To belong to God's family is the better way of living a life that includes and welcomes every single person, and every culture identity is welcomed to the Way and Word of God.

Chapter Six

Financial

"Greatness is not what you have, it is what you give." Unknown

"No one can serve two masters, for either he will hate the one and love the other, or he will be devoted to the one and despise the other. You cannot serve God and money." Mt. 6:24.

"Keep your lives free from the love of money and be content with what you have, because God said, "never will I leave you; never will I forsake you." Hebrew 13:5.

Money from every country and source of currency has imprinted famous leaders on it, colors of ink and standard markings that differentiate the tender and hopefully make it hard to counterfeit or cheapen its value.

It lies there in paper and coin as objects that only have purpose of usage and the provisions we activate upon exchange for services, and goods purchased to supply what we need to house our families, feed and clothe ourselves and others, medical and educational demands, travel expenditures, and exposures to moral/ethical dispositions exposed by the attitude we hold about money and use money.

Our inclinations about money are like a spiritual thermometer revealing how healthy or sick we are with God, Self/Soul, and Others. Scripture offers us thousands of verses around money. Money determines our wealth status, our willingness around giving, or withholding money because of values, ethics, complex psych social and spiritual effects on our character and attitude. The power to misuse money to the detriment of another human being. The power to share or give money to the salvation and wellbeing needs of another human being. There is more said about money in scripture of Old/New Testament than the topics of love and faith and fear.

We are invited by God to see what a valuable asset we are in our own uniquely and wonderfully made essence. We come with skills and talents we can hone. There are natural aptitudes we can bring into relationships with family, friends, and broader community to be a part of doing life together. Talents, resources, and assets given and shared assist in giving us all a place and opportunity to meet needs.

Financial health is not about being on some socio-economic wealth status from the low, middle, or high income determined by our own Western Cultures defining. We are shaped and often trapped in the comparison concerns, cost of living, job losses and hindrances from setbacks. Those setbacks and interferences that come with financial struggles always come with a story and circumstances when need is higher than monetary availability. The loss job, medical diagnosis, overspending, hoarding, impulsiveness, over giving, speculation, greed, inheritances, and charity all have a story to tell in the object and subject of money.

In every story there is a complexity of multiple strands of encountering one's own self/soul and the self/soul of another's character and attitude in how they see this hot topic of finances. Marriages, families, and siblings are eroded away by it or helped by it. Using money determines clubs, communities, groups, and friendships we affiliate with. The support of nonprofits, tithes and charities rely on the sharing of our charitable dollars to improve the lives of others less fortunate than ourselves in those charities, ministries and missions.

Money exposes the stories which reveal an inspiration of survival, perseverance from tragedy to triumph, kindness instead of greed, generosity over misuse of power, love rather than judgmentalism, peace of contentment instead of egotism, self-control over impulsiveness, goodness of forbearance instead of mean spiritedness of arrogance, long suffering of rebuilding after a natural disaster, patience in loss of independence and medical diagnosis, wisdom of contentment rather than comparison traps, joy of giving without an agenda of using another, and faithfulness to regard others rather than neglecting another or others.

These fruits of spirit and character traits infused in how we address the usage, excesses and depletions of money reveal the spiritual ethics of how we treat God, self/soul, and others.

Money is a neutral commodity that is a spiritual mirror about us. God is not neutral however about having a love of money before our love for God. There are people so well off and rich with money, yet they are poor. There are people with extraordinarily little or get by with just enough money who are very content with God, self/soul, and others who know they are rich.

The love of money is the root of all evil (I Timothy 6:10). Remember our conversation around the word 'love'. Love is not an emotion. Love is the active catalyst that moves an individual to feed an emotion that is exposed in either a negative or positive usage. Loving money is the beginning of feeding and reflecting a dark pleasure taken in misuse of power, pride, and the purposes which often are creating harm and havoc to not only the erosion of one's own soul/self but often the impact of harm on others.

Think of Scrooges character in Dickens *A Christmas Carol*. Think family splits over inheritances and wills contested. Think about the headlines of Hollywood moguls, CEOs, Politicians in the pockets of lobbyists, foreign special interest deals, embezzlement stories, and purchases of human beings for sex trafficking. Think price gauging after a disaster. Think about the wake of hurt and harm done to so many souls, all for the love of money. These examples are just a few.

- Money is a neutral tool and resource that also acts like a mirror in our lives, reflecting who we are at the core of our being.
- Money gives us an opportunity to be generous, kind, ethical, giving, and providing for needs to be met while living.
- Money educates, clothes, shelters, and feeds us.
- Money helps us celebrate and make memories of travel and time with others. The intent of the use and the agenda of why we use money is the spiritual thermometer God's Holy Spirit would want us to be aware of and attuned to for gratitude. Thanking God for what we have and how we use what we have is not about the amount in our bank account, or social-economic class.
- Money is not what we love. We love God and are grateful for all levels and layers of provisions.
  Scripture
- "For there will never cease to be poor in the land; that is why I am commanding you to open wide your hand to your brother and to the poor and needy in your land." Deuteronomy 15:11.
- "Aware of this, Jesus asked, "Why are you bothering this woman? She has done a beautiful deed to Me. The poor you will always have with you, but you will not always have me." Matt. 26:10.
- "My brothers and sisters, believers in our glorious Lord Jesus Christ, must not show favoritism. Suppose a man

comes into your meeting wearing a gold ring and fine clothes, and a poor man in filthy old clothes also comes in. If you show special attention to the man wearing fine clothes and say, "Here's a good seat for you," but say to the poor man, "You stand there" or "Sit on the floor by my feet," have you not discriminated among yourselves and become judges with evil thoughts? Listen, my dear brothers and sisters: Has not God chosen those who are poor in the eyes of the world to be rich in faith and to inherit the kingdom he promised those who love him? But you have dishonored the poor. Is it not the rich who are exploiting you? Are they not the ones who are dragging you into court? Are they not the ones who are blaspheming the noble name of him to whom you belong? If you really keep the royal law found in Scripture, "Love your neighbor as yourself," you are doing right. But if you show favoritism, you sin and are convicted by the law as lawbreakers." James 2: 1-9.

These few verses and a few bible characters such as the Rich Young Ruler, Judas, Zacchaeus, and the Widow and her Mite are a few opportunities to see the first three had money as an idol in their life and the Widow who was poor gave everything, she had to honor God. Zacchaeus will repent this mistake and make a new attitude change around serving God with his money.

Scripture from Old and New Testament speak to a spiritual discipline of giving that helps support the missions, ministries, and expenditures of running a faith community. The term tithe from the Old Testament means 10% of one's income. The New Testament speaks to tithing without self-righteousness in one's attitude, The New Testament speaks of giving of first fruits, don't turn away from someone in need, be generous, and cheerful in our giving. But a literal percentage or giving as a way of bribing God to bless us is not in Jesus' teaching of worshipping God. The Holy Spirit is our New Testament gift from God at Pentecost and will guide us in our giving of money, time, and the attitude from which to do so for the community of faith needs, and support of those in need.

Some teachers and scholars of the Sermon on the Mount remind us this is the new law building on the Ten Commandments from the Old Testament. To follow the words of Jesus in the Beatitudes listed in the Sermon on the Mount is to realize that the Ten Commandments is a legalized list of guidelines for holy living. Still valid but Jesus builds on an inner heart disposition it would take to live out the Beatitudes reveal holy living will take everything you've got every day to fulfill this Sermon's way of holy living. We need grace to strive to heed those standards.

Thus, with money not being our idol, and higher standards in our spiritual disciplines we are challenged to give time and money to care for the missions and ministry needs of poor, widows, health, benevolence, charity and care of others as mandated and encouraged by Jesus' words in Matthew 5. Let us be salt and light in a hurting world and glorify God with our abilities, assets, time, and money. The Non-Profit Source, offers stats that report:

- 60% are willing to give to their church digitally.

- Tithers make up only 10-25 percent of a normal congregation.

- Churches that accept tithing online increase overall donations by 32%.

- Only 5% tithe, and 80% of Americans only give 2% of their income.

- Christians are giving at 2.5% of income; during the Great Depression it was 3.3%.

- For families making $75k+, 1% of them gave at least 10% in tithing.

- 3 out of 4 people who don't go to church make donations to nonprofit organizations.

- About 10 million tithers in the US donate $50 billion yearly to church & non-profits.

- 77% of those who tithe give 11%–20% or more of their income, far more than the baseline of 10%.

- 7 out of 10 tithers do so based on their gross and not their net income.

Under Pandemic conditions of 2020 many nonprofits have suffered from loss of opportunities to fundraise and provide the special events of galas, dinners, silent auctions, and marketing the cause of charitable support. However, the culture of the American spirit did show an uptick by 7.6% for small and mid-sized charitable organizations. The number of donors giving was also up by 11.7%. In December of 2020, the charity giving was around $2.47 billion dollars in donations according to Reuters.com article on giving trends.

The stats on giving to faith and charity in recent timelines gives hope and some insight that American's in faith and in this culture at large are in general a giving people.

We hear so much negative about our culture of American life. No culture, faith, or people are perfect in any place or space on the globe. The way we treat money and people will show us what is at the core of our culture and spirit. Average Americans are far more givers than takers even under the duress of a Pandemic. With all the challenging news and messages of America's shortcomings these stats are reflections of what is good and best about the spirit of us at the heart of us. God Bless us for willing to be givers in all times, but especially these times.

Chapter Seven

Vocational

"You did not choose me, but I chose you and appointed you should go and bear fruit and that your fruit should abide, so that whatever you ask the Father in my name, he may give it to you." John 15:16.

"Where the needs of the world meet your talents is your vocation." Aristotle.

"Wherever God had put, you are your vocation. It is not what we do but how much love we give it that matters." Mother Teresa.

"For I know the plans I have for you, declares the Lord, plans for welfare and not for evil, to give you a future and a hope." Jeremiah 29: 11.

We often speak of God's will for our lives with trepidation of fearing what God will ask of us. We have an element of ignorance and naivety that God is only interested in our big decisions in life and never the small choices we address. Throughout the narratives in Old Testament and New we meet a God that encourages a relationship of trust that God's own will is good for us and will give us directions through discerning conversations of prayer time with the Holy One.

The Holy One is a sovereign God as Isaiah 46: 9-10 offer: "I am God, and there is no other; I am God, and there is none like me, declaring the end from the beginning and from ancient times things not yet done, saying, my counsel shall stand, and I will accomplish all my purpose."

This is encouraging to build trust with a God who Jesus modeled for us to say, 'your will and not mine.' When we trust God, our concerns can rest in no fear and contentment that God shows up to help us with our vocational occupational and daily duties that demand much of our time and talents. The labels we wear in so many attributes of a vocational calling are more than the title of the work we do for a paycheck.

While that is certainly a part of God's will and interest in our life. God is interested in all efforts and labels of work we live with in the 24/7 duties of our day, and the year in and year out list of efforts we strive to provide for our families, care of others, and self/soul care individually too. God's will is involved and interested in everything about us.

Relating to the Holy One in prayer, knowledge of Him in scripture, awareness of the modeling and messages from Jesus' ministry will aid us in the understanding of God's will for our lives in every decision we address, including our vocation of work.

Often, we argue with God about our limitations. There is a lacking we feel we have to do a certain vocational work or calling. With prayerful discernment of God's Holy Spirit, we press on and prepare. Then God makes a way and moves us from one moment to the next.

What I understand about God's will in my life:

- Is that not everyone will agree with what God and I have agreed upon and even had a covenant of our own between us in prayer.
- There is no easy street to the journey of any vocation or calling or label we wear in this lifetime. There has been nothing simplistic about becoming a minister that is female. It is all good today, but the journey was a lot of wilderness wandering, blocked access to seminary, and challenges from the powerful sources that did not make inclusion or encouragement a part of the journey starting in 1979. But, in my gut and in my bones, I knew what God and I agreed upon in efforts of pastoral care and call for assisting souls in healthy faith and healthy family dynamics, especially when under times of crisis and duress.
- God gives me an amazing peace and certainty that is hard to put into words and encourages me to stay the course.
- Trust and Freewill are the principal ingredients in the decisions around vocation and labels lived within God's will and mine, finding a harmony and contentment without fear allows for freedom.
- When doors have closed, and another could have invested or encouraged the vocational journey of me but doesn't or hasn't; the Holy One gives me freedom to cry out what I must, dust myself off, and listen to the Spirit about another way. Six decades later I can honestly say what has not worked out and those who have not believed in my vocational calling was a positive for my journey. It has been a lifetime of amazing experiences with God's care and directions of navigating have been outstanding.

The doors of this vocation in pastoral care, grief support, and counseling in chaplaincy duties have been my honor. There have been colleagues, leaders, and national leadership in areas of healthcare and multiple faith denominations that have been amazing supporters and sojourners with me on this ministry journey. What a delight to know them and be known by them as we served, advocated, taught, and helped in thousands of death stories in end-of-life work. Since 2005, the amazing experiences with God's care and directions of navigating have been outstanding in this season too.

It is about honing our holiness edges in our own soul/self. It is not about happiness, wealth, health, and giving us our way on our terms.

The journey of occupations and vocations lives in more than what we do for a living, and more than any label we have worn. This includes any label of work, time, money, and talent we offered in our family of origin, in our own family life made in another generation. We are more than our dreams dashed, our dreams fulfilled, limitations or no limitations.

Truly, we human-divine souls are more than the labels we have worn in each season of our lives. Those labels however have been influential teachers for relating to God, knowing ourselves/soul better and revealing others in their labels too. It is a complex and messy mix of interconnectedness from which we strive, thrive, and survive what makes us choose who we want to become in the utilization of our own freewill.

Finally, God's will for us in living bold lives, in our timeline of life, while we are here is for our own soul/self to become like Christ. As a Jesus follower we are always working out our own salvation of maturing in the faith, praying with discernment, seeking God's will to be ours naturally too. It is trust and abiding love which anchors us in this life and the next life to a Holy One in Three and Three in One that loves us more than we can fathom but we can trust.

Now life is not fair. That is a foundational truth since the dawn of time. It does rain on the just and unjust. Matt. 5:45 reminds, "that you may be children of your Father in heaven. He causes his sun to rise on the evil and the good and sends rain on the righteous and the unrighteous."

If we think being good, praying and begging hard enough, and being fair to others is going to give us some edge of favor with the Holy One to spare us from grief, loss, and unfairness in our own lives we are very shallow, mistaken, and naïve about who God is and who we are as one of God's own.

Down through the ages of history human isms of treatment to one another should tell us something about this level of unfairness. Was it fair that Hagar had to be involved with Sarah and Abraham's efforts to have a baby? Was it fair for Judah to ignore the pleas of fairness per their own culture towards Tamar? Was it fair to over tax much of society from ancient governments to present governments? Was it fair to have a system of slavery and indentured servants in every culture across the globe in our human history? Was it fair to limit the value of women, people of color, or differing ethnicities as less than capable to fulfill a certain role of work?

How many minds, talents, and offerings of worth to our human family have gone wasted, unutilized, or underutilized because of our human need to limit one another in those ism's we employed?

No one gets a pass of judging the past per our mindsets today. History does not need our 21st century opining opinions. What we need to heed; is the present changes needed and remaining ethics of good and trustworthy traditions worth keeping. But that takes serious levels of prayer and discernment from those prayers with God to know the plumb line God is looking for from us on our timeline of life.

We will all be history soon enough. The quest within the question is this: "Is the world a better place because we are here?" "Would you want you for a boss, employee, friend, relative, sibling, spouse, parent, child, or neighbor?" Every role and label we occupy and job we do in any label is worth reflecting on the contributions we bring to the timeline of life from which we live.

There is a quote that I value highly in this topic of vocation and value of labels worn. Rabbi Zusya was an Orthodox Rabbi that died in 1800 in the Ukraine. He was lamenting and challenging up to his last days about his life reflections on his work while he was here on earth. His students asked him why he morns after all the excellent work he did in his lifetime. We need a little back story in order to grasp this quote.

Judaism in the Talmud teaches the importance of being like Moses. Yet, Deuteronomy 34:10 of the Torah (Old Testament) states, "no one is as great as Moses." So, Rabbi Zusya laments that when he goes before God in heaven, he knows God will not ask him why he was not more like Moses or even King David. God is going to ask of him, "why were you not more like Zusya?"

God fills us all with giftedness, talents, and abilities that are clues and opportunities of our vocational and occupational and personal labels of offerings to the world we serve while we are here. The sad truth we must hear is that often talents and skills are treasures we will bury in the dust of history because of the many ism's humanity projects and costs everyone. When I was a child, we sang a song entitled, *This Little Light of Mine*. The message was that we are all asked to shine because the world needs our gifts. This is not about fame, money, or prestige. The message is about the talents and skills and love we can offer one another while we are here for our turn around the sun of time. However long we live, did we bring our best self/soul to the table of living while we were here?

But, if there are roadblocks, hinderances, and setbacks, then we wonder if the efforts to fulfill such endeavors are ever forthcoming. The many ism's down through history have shifted the needle of unfairness some and improvements have taken place. With no need to condemn the past or chastise cultural, gender, ethnic, and economic ism's because it is such a waste of time and no one is innocent of ism's selfish behaviors.

How we perform our work with ethics, attitude, and effort will reveal the fruit of our own character addressing any isms within ourselves. Jesus reminds us in Matt. 7:3, "Why do you look at the speck of sawdust in your brother's eye and pay no attention to the plank in your own eye?" There is so much need for self-awareness and self-ownership in our own well-examined life. If we did such spiritual work on our own self/soul maturing the ism's in a fallen world, just might lessen statistically. Will we reach some utopian egalitarian universe? Not on this side of heaven's gates, but it can get better with honest self/soul awareness efforts.

It took me nearly 30 years to get to walk into a seminary and begin the calling of pastoral care work that God laid on my heart in 1979. The challenges of what a minister can do or become given their femininity was no small feat to complete. When I entered seminary in 2001, most of the students were only a few years older than my own children. What I knew about my journey, through prayer, was that God's Spirit pushed me to never give up. God also called my best friend into ministry work in the late 1980s and after a decade of my challenges tucked into my story; I was worried for her. It also frustrated me at the reality of how little this female minister attribute had changed in our own culture of American life, built on freedoms and equality essences espoused but not always a reality.

Today, we have both accomplished serving in ministry for over fifteen years. We may not get to do all we are capable of or wanted to do, but we got to be the female ministers in the veins and ways God has provided for us both in this vocational calling. We both have had a challenging time and a beautiful journey that is rich in gratitude that we ever even got to do ministry at all.

Today, it is easy to focus mostly on the negative that gets messaged on holdbacks and roadblocks in our lives. Truth of the matter is that it does rain on the just and unjust. Life situations can be unfair. No one owes us our way on our terms, but we all get the opportunity to try, to pursue, to begin, or to strive for our vocations/occupations we desire to accomplish.

Today, we both keep moving forward to the next chapter God has for us in these days of service and vows to our ministerial calling that rests between us and God.

There is a prayer from Mother Teresa that feeds my own Spirit in this issue of vocational calling. The prayer is entitled,

Anyway

People are often unreasonable, irrational, and self-centered.

Forgive them anyway.

If you are kind, people may accuse you of selfish, ulterior motives.

Be kind anyway.

If you are successful, you will win some unfaithful friends and some genuine enemies. Succeed, anyway.

If you are honest and sincere, people may deceive you.

Be honest and sincere anyway.

What you spend years creating, others could destroy overnight.

Create anyway.

If you find serenity and happiness, some may be jealous.

Be happy anyway.

The good, you do today will often be forgotten.

Do good anyway.

Give the best you have, and it will never be enough.

Give your best anyway.

In the final analysis, it is between you and God.

It was never between you and them anyway.

Rabbi Zusya and Mother Teresa in their own way are saying the same thing. We must be us and answer to God for how well we lived out our own authentic and genuine lives fully and well for God,

Self/Soul, and Others by being the best us we could be on the timeline of history while we were here.

Our vocation is not about money, titles, accomplishments, and approval standards set by others. Our race and pace of our vocational lives are between us and God. I will not get some blue ribbon or gold watch for how many books I wrote, funerals and end-of-life care given, grief care and counseling given, bible studies offered, or sermons done or ungiven. God is more interested around the issues of:

- Did I say yes and give it my all?
- Did I trust Him along the way?
- Did I enjoy and learn from both sides of life's reality of what is good and not good but kept going with gratitude for both, anyway?
- Did I keep growing, giving, gathering, and being my best?
- Did I strive to pass on God's love and message to others?
- Did I lie down and quit or get out of the abyss that tried to swallow me up?
- Did I live out the story of me to my fullest endeavor?

These are the reflection questions that reveal the quest of me (and you) as we travel this world on our timeline of life in the here and now.

Prayer and poetry are valuable wordings and phrases I gather from for inspiration. In Mary Oliver's poem When Death Comes there is a section of wording that moves me in this poetry:

"When it's over, I want to say all my life I was a bride married to amazement. I was the bridegroom, taking the world into my arms. When it is over, I don't want to wonder if I have made of my life something particular and real. I don't want to find myself sighing and frightened or full of argument. I don't want to end up simply having visited this world."

The work we do matters. The talents and gifts of us we bring to the world matters. The efforts of care through our many jobs are more than a paycheck. The attitude in which we move in our work matters. The gratitude and ethics we offer in our vocational duties matters.

Our occupation and vocation of work rests on our aptitude and abilities to do the work required. The disposition and fruit of spirit used in the functions of our work is the foundation that matters most.

To die with regret, guilt, unfinished business, unforgiveness, and apathy or hatred for another is a waste of God's precious gift of life.

When death comes

like the hungry bear in autumn;

when death comes and takes all the bright coins from his purse

to buy me, and snaps the purse shut;

when death comes

like the measle-pox

when death comes

like an iceberg between the shoulder blades,

I want to step through the door full of curiosity, wondering:

what is it going to be like, that cottage of darkness?

And therefore I look upon everything

as a brotherhood and a sisterhood,

and I look upon time as no more than an idea,

and I consider eternity as another possibility,

and I think of each life as a flower, as common

as a field daisy, and as singular,

and each name a comfortable music in the mouth,

tending, as all music does, toward silence,

and each body a lion of courage, and something precious to the earth.

When it's over, I want to say all my life

I was a bride married to amazement.

I was the bridegroom, taking the world into my arms.

When it's over, I don't want to wonder

if I have made of my life something particular, and real.

I don't want to find myself sighing and frightened,

or full of argument.

I don't want to end up simply having visited this world (By: Mary Oliver)

Chapter Eight

Last Things

This read began with first things first. The quest in the journey of a spiritual life lived boldly and well begins with some questions. The answer to those questions opens up the quest we will live out within our life by the answers to those questions.

- How was God introduced to you?
- What is your image of God that you believe, value, do not believe, do not value?
- Is God involved in all the facets and compartmentalization's of your one wonderful life? How?
- What are the prayer conversations between you and God, like in the daily routine of living out your life?
- How do scripture and understandings of God's movement inform you about the Holy One you walk and talk with in routine life?
- Is the Holy Spirit of God able to get your attention during these conversations of prayer and transform you in listening and discerning God's movement in your life together?

- Do you look for God in the daily moments of your day with openness to communicate, give gratitude, and/or deepen the relationship?
- When your life here is over and time is no longer relevant for you; are you leaving a legacy of love and positive contributions in all the labels in life you lived out with others?

I have been a social worker, chaplain, grief counselor, pastoral care minister to staff, teacher, writer, traveler, marketer, and business owner. I have been a wife, mother, sister, daughter, friend, neighbor, and lifelong student. I have been creative and active with prayer poetry, photography, decorating, fishing, golf, crafts, puzzles, word and card games. All these areas have taught me something about God's movement in the world, my self/soul awareness, others, and the variety of systems I have interacted with along the way. Along life's peaks, valleys, and routine roads, each person, decade, and each system I interacted with taught me something about encountering God, my own self/soul, and others. Yet, nothing is more the great equalizer to life than to deal with death and dying stories. I have held decades of stories of crisis, loss, laments, and death in my duties and work along this journey.

Many of the stories I have witnessed held the confidential needs and performed the funerals, which have held a few reality checks. No one gets through this life without loss, deep griefs, betrayals, setups, and setbacks. Each human-divine soul comes into this life on a timeline of history that forms them and informs them along way. With freewill, values, beliefs, and ethics that reflect who they were as they moved in this world with the God of their understanding, personality, talents, opportunities, reactions and responses to the interconnection and impact that family, faith, experiences, and choices made had on them. This is not to simplify what is actually complex in the making of a human-divine self/soul.

However, each of us enters this world with absolutely nothing and we did absolutely nothing to arrive here for the journey. What we get to do with the gift of life is to choose and determine exactly how we are going to live out the life God has given each of us regardless of the arrival, family, genetics, nurtured, or nature circumstances.

If our lives and very humanity are made in the image of God, then getting to know this God on an intimate level will only benefit us. There is a vast Mystery to God. The Trinity attributes in Christian Spirituality helps us walk and talk with a God we cannot put in a box and make claims we own this God as a personal servant giving us our way if we pray right enough and are good enough people in our own eyes. God is holy and so sovereign and such a Mystery; it is us that are subjects to this God. It is us that owes God our gratitude that we were even born at all. God's gift of life is a gift, and our gift back to God is in how we chose to live out this life with and for God. This Creator God owes no one and none of us our way on our terms in this life.

We are drawn to God's majesty and sovereignty out of instinct for something beyond ourselves. Then we find God's ways are higher than our own. "God's ways are as mysterious as the pathway of the wind and as the manner in which a human spirit is infused into the little body of a baby while it is yet in its mother's womb." Eccl. 11:5.

Dr. A. W. Tozer was a gifted preacher and prophet of his day. Over a half a century ago he warned the systems of organized evangelical churches to stop grieving the Holy Spirit by not allowing the Spirit of God to be the real Lord of the church rather than humankind's selfish and self-serving agendas. In his book, "Man's Pursuit of God", Tozier points to the three ways we can seek and know God, up to a point. First through worship, through the Gospel and introduction of Jesus' teaching, "If you know Me, you will also know My Father. From now on you know Him and have seen Him" (John 14:7). And we come to accept our limitations and know 'God' through the examinations through scriptures. For some scriptures, there are hard sayings offered, and outcomes of God's responses are limiting for humankind. We will never fully explain all things about God. We know enough and truthfully, we human/divine beings can hardly handle what we do know about God.

There is an acknowledgment here that we humans need to worship and acknowledge something of awe in the Divine we named God. Yet, there is something about God that is so holy and beyond our full knowing that we accept we must put our rationalizations and explanations to rest. We who are the created will not fully explain the majesty and mystery of a holy God.

There is a Divine Transcendence of God no denomination or religion can hold all the answers to explain the mind of God. Jesus is the Word made flesh that offers us a glimpse but reminds us, "who has known the mind of the Lord so as to instruct him? But we have the mind of Christ." I Cor. 2:16.

From the Torah, Wisdom Books of Scripture, Minor and Major Prophets of the Old Testament, we can study the character and interaction of God with humankind. Likewise, in the words and wisdom offerings of the Apocrypha, and the Gospel and New Testament writings: repeatedly we see a Creator that creates out of the chaos and freewill choices of human/divine beings who have messy and marvelous lives to share with us generation after generation.

If God has given us spiritual attributes to our humanity, then we have our work cut out to grow our spiritual wellbeing to its best within us as we strive to invest in improving our humanity/divinity with understanding, education, interaction with others, care of our physical bodies, mastery of emotions vetted, using our gifts and talents in occupational and vocational offerings, attitude with money, disposition and awareness of various cultural influences, the socializing, associates and friendships we keep. Do we live lives worth having, a faith worth passing on to the next generation, and a foundation of spiritual wellness in our human/divine makeup?

Stories

In my six decades and forty-plus years of work, there have been thousands of stories that have crossed with mine and the labels I have worn in the interaction. I have learned much from scripture, life's experiences, and studies. However, the most profound lessons were from the dying.

One of these stories was a woman of 90 something. She was from a rural part of Georgia and lived a lifetime of running a farm and being a dutiful wife and daughter. Typical of many Southern families, a firstborn was expected to help the family business and give a great part of their time even in adulthood to making the needs of the matriarch and patriarch of family life function easily and sufficiently alongside any family life they may have had of their own.

There were no conversations around boundaries, age stage appropriateness for adult-to-adult relating's, or courtesy of their concerns in most given circumstances. Boundary lines in many families of the South are blurred extremely, and it had and has its damaging effects on a person's personal soul care; not to mention the marriages and family dynamics of the next and next generations this type of cultural nuances costs and ripples into those next generations. Self/soul awareness can become compromised and the development of wholeness and wellness can go dormant into unfinished business, immaturity, naiveness, and unfulfilled use of the individual's talent and contribution as limited. This woman shared that she would have liked to have been a nurse. Nurses in her day were single and not allowed to be a nurse once they married.

This was the outcome of a woman who was married for over 50 years and never ventured more than a trip to the beach, downtown Atlanta, or Birmingham, Alabama in her ninety years. She told me she had no children; she felt fortunate because she got to finish high school and never held a job beyond helping her parents run their farm and manning a farmer's market. She loved her life; her husband was an honorable man, and she missed him every day she had to go on without him after he died. When we had our pastoral care and time together, she was always positive, quick-witted with a great sense of humor, and missed being able to do her crafts and needlepoint work. She would take some of her work to the farmers' market and display them for sale and orders from customers looking for doilies and lace she had tatted. The ability to tat lace is a lost art to us today.

She had taken a turn for the worse. She refused to eat or drink, and there was a significant decline, but the nursing home staff sensed she was hanging on for some unspoken reason. So, they asked her if there was someone they could call, and she wanted to see her chaplain. So, they called me to come give her last prayers and find out what is keeping her here if she is refusing to eat and drink and succumbing to the bodies decline.

When I walked in the room, she looked like she had already passed. Lying in that bed extremely pale, and one had to pay close attention to spot that breathing was still there but very shallow. I took her hand, and she gave me a slight grin that took a lot of effort. Holding people's stories is sacred work. Giving them a safe place to land on safer ears and to be known is a privilege. Helping God's children birth their soul's back to Him is no small feat. In that moment I sense she had a sacred, important story of her own she needed to let go of and it honored me to hear it and be a witness to her life's journey.

With some whispered efforts and clarifications between us, the words rolled out to reveal she had a daughter. She was born and died the same day in a home birth at the family farm she served for all her life. Her husband and mother would not let her hold the dying child, nor name her. She laid in her birthing state for hours, crying to see her baby. Her husband took the baby away and did not tell her where on the farm he buried his child by himself. He only assured her they would have another and not to speak of this loss. They never had another child. She wanted me to know he could not face the grief. Not talking was his way of moving beyond the loss. She needed to forgive her mother for demanding they not name the baby. And it was her mother that demanded she and her husband 'get over it by burying it and never talking about it.' So, in a matriarchal Southern cultural moment, that is what they did.

It is hard to describe the essence of sacred sharing of that moment back then into this moment of writing and witnessing her death bed need to leave this story with someone. The mix of a time in life that is not my own, for she entered this world in 1918. However, a culture of Southerner's that had its roots in mine was alerting. The faith of hard, stoic Scots-Irish Baptist that run a farm was also a part of my heritage, and yet I was the first real generation to be freer from such and yet not really. In that moment, I realized she needed me to know something dear and secret about her and from her own words.

The encounter made me aware of the tentacle of the million or more Southern stories that have this element of stoicism in grief, hard resilience to cling to family that had poor boundaries and regards for the next generations marriages and life pursuits, and females had very little voice or power except through the expectations to honor the matriarch or the patriarch without a peep if one were to keep the peace. In the tension of this revelation, I asked her to tell me what she named her baby girl. "Emma, I named her Emma, and I cannot leave this world without someone knowing I was her mother." She also wanted to know if I thought Emma would know her in heaven. "Yes, she will I said."

The space between us was like a suspended limbo of peace, grace, forgiveness, confession, and hope all rolled up into one overwhelming sacred encounter. Prayers given, she went back to a restful state with eyes closed and thanking me for being her pastor at the end of her days. I left, knowing this would most likely be my last visit with her alive. Her voice was weak but still with her, so I thought she might have another day or two. Strong wills in the human spirit have never ceased to amaze me in this end-of-life work. This time together was in the morning, and by the time the 5pm dinner had come to her in her room, she was gone. The facility called and thanked me for giving her the peace to be with God. I knew God was introducing her to the daughter she finally got to hold and see her Emma.

In my end-of-life work, I witnessed the ones who died well and peacefully had a few things in common:

- They held a disposition of peace with God, self, and others.
- They put to rest the ghosts of regrets with forgiveness.
- They learned from their life journey how to be resilient and face disappointments with emotional intelligence and maturity of faith in God.
- The most common factor of those who died well were those who loved well and whole in their days of living.

In end-of-life work I have witnessed stories of those who died with unfinished business, confessions of regrets, and held onto anger from some story of long ago. These more negative losses and influential tragedies left the dying more restless and fretful in the dying process. This taught me how congruent both life and death are with each other. Often, we will die the way we live. If each day we live is ladened in fretfulness, full of angst, regrets, anger, denials, lies we tell ourselves to be the victim, hero, or martyr in some drama story of long ago those rocks will pile on in the death story at the end too. Each person who comes or remains absent at the death story of the dying patient has a side from which they are speaking. Yet only God knows the details of the truth and what it means in the complexity of the stories involved.

Usually, there is little to do in the shifting of a storyline that has gone on too long and it remains too entrenched in its dysfunctional elements of immature emotions, and inability to forgive what needs forgiving or too heinous a story that only God can help supernaturally in the forgiveness work. When a story is so heinous, and the rifts are vastly stretching to the soul injuries done then the spiritual work of forgiving and growing out of losses can be done but without reconciliation and reengaging in doing life together. The efforts for reconciliation are a waste of time in such storylines. However, there are many stories that are very capable of reengaging and reconciling when each involved is willing to utilize spiritual disciplines of a maturing faith, emotional resilience, authentic awareness, and honest regret for any part played in the harming through words or deeds. If there is only more or the same patterns and behaviors then each is better off forgiving and loving one another from afar, but no longer able to be in a relationship that enjoys doing life together.

Sadly at the death, the trap of time running out is up, and both parties lose the opportunity to make peace with God-Self/Soul-Others. There are no winners in these stories. This is not an honorable way to live, and it does not lead to a good death for anyone involved in the storyline of family and friend dynamics at end of life.

Another story

One of those stories was a man who had been a Veteran and fought in Vietnam. Actually, I have several Veteran stories that have this similar thread in the weaving of a life. However, this man had come home from the war rather broken and wounded from the inside out and in nearly every area of what we have striven to compartmentalize for convenience's sake in living boldly physically, emotionally, vocationally, culturally, financially, socially, and within it all the use or no use for a spiritual compass in all compartments.

This man had PTSD (post-traumatic stress disorder) and went deeply inward and rarely spoke to anyone in his return home from Vietnam. However, he functioned enough to marry a girl he knew in high school and they had a daughter. This first wife divorced him and took their daughter away and started life over with someone else less broken than him. After a few years of living with his parents as an only adult child, he could complete some schooling that put him in a quiet office as an accountant. He even married again. He married a woman with two children from another marriage and he became an excellent stepfather that these two never felt was a stepfather.

To these two children he was their proper father. He remained a quiet, unassuming man and his second wife abused him. We don't hear too much about women abusing men and pushing them into a place of nothingness in domestic violence of words, neglect, gaslighting, and physical harm. He eventually had a stroke and became paralyzed on one side. His speech was mildly affected, and he would talk with his stepdaughter in brief and limited words of effort. He refused to talk to nursing staff or hospice staff or anyone through a form of selective mutism. Selective mutism is a form of server anxiety. He would freeze and flee inward for protection. The stepdaughter had medical and financial responsibility for him and even had a medical and legal order that her own mother could not visit and create any drama for him.

Through a program of We Honor Veterans, our team found him a Veteran volunteer to come and try to gain some peace for him in this family dynamic, Vietnam, persona of fragility, and withdrawal. It worked. The Veteran volunteer could pull him into a place of camaraderie around similar stories and need to make him feel safe with his own. He still had selective mutism, but with nodding and a keyboard he would poke letters and wordings to get his own voice out and make his needs known. There were a few wins in his end-of-life story. There was no tidy bow of all is well and everyone was in a happily ever after outcome. He did consent to see his daughter from the first marriage, and it seemed to give her more closure than it did for him. His stepson stopped coming because it was too hard for him to see him in such a physical state, and that affected the patient greatly and sadly. The stepdaughter and the Veteran volunteer were the bravest and steadiest pair of good care for the patient's mind, body, spirit balance. Their presence and protection of his emotions was outstanding.

The last thing I could do for him was feed him his pureed food at lunch and prayer with him. He typed out on his keyboard a request for me to give him communion. I agreed and scheduled it for the following week. It was a first for me to bless the elements of bread mashed with thickening liquid and grape juice with thickening. We found our way and humor in the awkwardness of drooling and pooling the elements with scriptures spoken in smiles and giggles to lighten our way through the challenge. He punched on the keyboard afterwards, 'piece of cake.'

About another week later, this patient died peacefully in his sleep in the early morning hours. No one by his bedside. No warning that there were any signs of imminent decline. He simply slipped away in his sleep peacefully. The stepdaughter had him buried in a military cemetery with graveside services only. Four people were there to witness his burial and pay homage for the service to our country. Vietnam took him into a dark and ugly time at 19 years of age. He lived most of his life stuck in a story that played over and over like a broken record as it broke him in so many spaces of himself. People left him in his stuckness. Some abused him in his stuckness, and others tried to befriend and succeeded. May he be in peace now.

The death stories are too many to offer all the lessons they leave behind for us all to learn from if we have eyes to see and ears to hear. Even the hardest deaths with so many twists and turns of family dynamics and unfinished wishes spelled out there is a need to accomplish one thing.

- **How do we give our fellow human-divine beings a death that has dignity?**

Dying well is really about living well. The only person who can claim what a good death is comes from the person dying. They are the ones who get to define their idea of a good death that has meaning for them. In life we do our own self determination and meaning making around hobbies and interest, college, wedding plans, making the nursery for the new baby, building or buying a home, or building a life that suits our habits and wishes. Why do we allow ourselves the luxury of choices in life but not make a single firm decision about how we want our death and dying experience to become?

Denial behaviors in life will be a culprit of chaos in death. Lack of acceptance of reality in living will also play a huge role in how well one accepts loss in a job, a divorce, a betrayal, a loss of health, loss of independence, and even the inevitable deaths that come into our story. Negative dispositions and controlling demeanors in life will show up darkly and with rude awakenings in death and dying stories. Positive determination with humor and hope will make both life and death reveal the gift of respect and rapport with others who must sojourn with you.

We only have one life and one death to complete. Respect for both will bring the spiritual fruit outcomes we spent so much time on in chapter one on spirituality layers of love, joy, peace, forbearance/long suffering, kindness, goodness, faithfulness, gentleness and self-control. The beginning and finishing well are paramount. Our lives messy middles are up to us to own and address with God's help through prayer and Holy Spirit discernment or not. That is our choice in the gift of freewill used in this one wonderful, wicked, terrible, tremendous, glorious, gory, fabulous and flawed lives we all get a chance at on a specific timeline in history.

I have lost count in fifteen years of chaplaincy duties of the many funerals done in end-of-life work. What I can offer in the lessons learned from these vast amounts of funerals and memorials is this:

- Most want to be remembered well and positively by their labels with family and friends.
- Most want to recount their value given if they served in the Armed Services.
- Most want their memory and eulogy to reflect humor, hard work, and personal interests and hobbies.
- Most want music that reflects their taste in both sacred and secular songs.
- Most want prayers, preaching, and pastors to keep their remarks short and not about fear of hell but the value of celebrating life and living well.
- Most want a video that captures memory making moments with family and friends.
- Most want to be remembered that they were here, and their life mattered to someone.

Most end-of-life stories hold to this norm and template of eulogizing. This is in keeping in which funerals support the living and witness the dead in a neutral to positive light. The saddest deaths I can recount are the ones where nearly no one comes or there is no memorial at all because there is no one left to come, even in a small group. Those deaths are the saddest ones. Many of these types simply outlived loved ones. Others lived lives of mental illness and limitations that they had become a ward of the state. Some fall in the cracks of forgotten and neglected by family, by no fault of their own.

Another story

One of my favorite souls I attended to was the oldest child of twelve. Grew up on a small farm in South Georgia. She helped her parents raise her siblings. She never talked about her brothers and sisters in details. She only found it strange that she would outlive every single one of them. She never married and stayed on the farm and took care of her aging parents until they passed away.

She was a choir leader in her church and sold her farm vegetables and canning goods at a farmers' market to make ends meet. She fainted one day in her own aging issues and the siblings talked her into selling the farm and splitting the money and sending her to a nursing home in Atlanta where they promised to visit and see her more.

She sold the farm and moved to Atlanta. She took to leading the choir and Sunday service participation at the nursing home. Over the years, her siblings died, and the family dwindled down to one nephew that checked on her once or twice a year. She never complained. She continued to espouse she found it strange that she was the oldest and outlived everyone. She was pragmatic and stoic and proud of her faith and roots of hard work. Whenever she saw me, she would say, "hey baby, you here for prayer with me?" She smiled a white, gorgeous smile for someone so aged, thin, and snow-white hair cropped close on her dark face. She looked like a sweet angel to me, and we had a beautiful friendship for over a decade together.

She was loved in her nursing home community too. She would be described as kind, laid back, quietly stoic, and also stubborn and determined. Similar descriptions I could give to my grandmother. She was from another era of time. African American in the South before integration and Civil Rights. She had seen her share of discrimination and sexism harms within her own community, family, and the white community against integration. She entered this world in 1918, just as my grandmother had in her Alabama lineage in the year 1917. Two women who had limited education, farm life, large families with their efforts to survive poverty and lack with gardens and farm animals to care for. What I came to admire about both women and their similar storylines was their resilience in their faith and generosity of rarely judging, complaining, or giving mean spirited criticism on those that harmed, neglected, and disrespected them along the way. They held those stories in some chasm of hope. Feeding others lots of excellent food was my grandmother's way. No longer able to have access to a kitchen, this other turned to Gospel music, recited favorite bible verses, and the guilty pleasure of smoking.

This sweet African American woman died several years after my grandmother died. I was determined to be by her bedside at her death, just as I had been with my own paternal grandmother. I was with her and sang an old Gospel hymn, 'Just as I Am' and then spent hours by her bedside letting Pandora play the rest of her favorite hymns.

She went peacefully while I was holding her hand, just as my grandmother had a few years earlier. She was indigent, and no family showed up to give her a burial or dignity of witnessing her life. So, I do that for her in this writing and in carrying her story with me in my heart. She is one of those stories that goes with me about the lack of dignity we do in our society with nameless paupers' graves. This was a self/soul that was rich in spirit, poor in money and no family left really to show up for her. This is one of those stories of one who died well, peacefully, in no pain, and someone who loved her was with her. But I still regret in our interconnectedness of paths crossing, I did not have the legal right or the money to claim how she would be buried. A social worker from the state would make those determinations. How sad that still makes me all these years later.

Dying with dignity and being buried with one's faith wishes is also a part of that dignity piece for our human-divine soul. We can do better, and I will keep advocating for such. Her story is a story of one who lived well against many challenging stories and circumstances and died well in her exit to join God's realms of heaven; but we in society did not do right, nor do we continue to do right when we bury the indigent, poor, and overlooked in undignified burial spaces like outcasts. She deserved better.

My story

The first time I realized I was a lover of stories; a holder of stories was forever ago. The gazillion seconds of 1,945,553,767 at this writing and since birth in 1959 has invested in the making of me and likewise I am sure your tick tock of time has made you too. We all have our beginning, middle, and inevitable end.

Thus, we are all a story and I have my favorites and not so favorites. There is the one about nearly drowning, the kidnapped story, the social worker stories: including the two stories where my life was threatened with a gun in my face. There are the education and certification journey stories, the surgery stories, the travels and living in foreign countries stories. The Southern family stories, the Military family stories, the treasured family stories and the broken family stories. The infertility days, the parenting season stories, the chronic pain stories, the cancer stories, the fishing stories, the golf stories, the sexist stories, the Florida State stories, the falling in love story, and the still in love story. There are the dog stories, the sports stories, the decorating stories, the church stories, the friendship stories, the ministry stories, the movie stories, and the music stories. The stories of me and of any of us cannot be measured by a single story. It takes the accumulation of all the stories and seasons of our life that help us get to know God, know ourselves, and know others through the interconnection of our stories together.

Final Word:

The ability to live well and die well and grieve well is from the spiritual muscles and wellness we embody with congruency of gratitude and grit. It has been my experience that even events of grief and good can happen in the same twenty-four hours together. How we hold and respond to both reflects who we are and reveals one another to each other in our encounters with one another. My prayer and hope are that this quest through the questions, scriptures, smattering of stories, and owning our spirituality in living, loss, death and dying experiences challenges us to know God deeper- gain self/soul awareness - offer the bread of life and light to another.

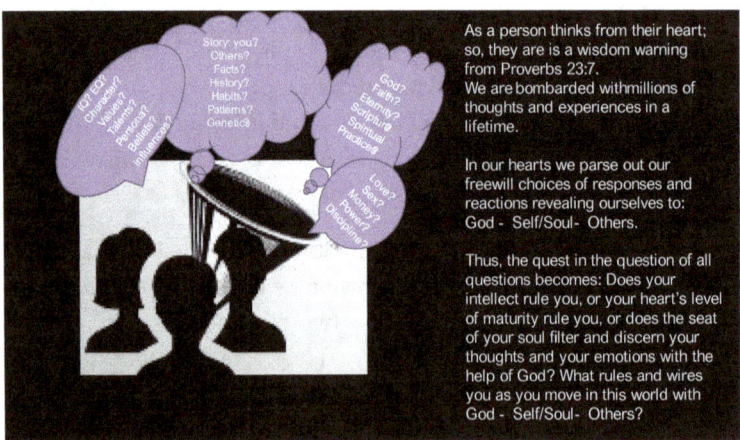

Peace and grace always, Dr. Deb.

www.ingramcontent.com/pod-product-compliance
Lightning Source LLC
Chambersburg PA
CBHW071454070526
44578CB00001B/339